WELCOME

Lasting approximately 45 years, the Cold War was a time of great change – politically, technologically, and militarily – and it saw the transformation of a world defined by World War Two to a new age of struggle, for post-colonial independence and for self-determination. Polarised and charged with suspicion, each side in the struggle for 'hearts and minds' overran the conventions of political and diplomatic behaviour through a banter of words and threats that tipped nuclear-armed states to the brink of self-annihilation through 'mutually assured destruction'.

Yet the push for technological virility symbols – on Earth and in space – brought benefits that would never have emerged as quickly as they did but for the pressure-cooker of national and international competition. Rockets designed for waging war were applied to the launch of satellites, providing improved weather warnings, global communications and television plus precise navigation and a world wide web. Computers and information storage and processing systems developed for the military brought connections for different groups around the world.

At times it produced great excitement as the first flight of the Anglo-French Concorde supersonic airliner and the first Moon landing by humans occurred in 1969, within less than five months of each other. While Concorde really had nothing to do with the Cold War, and the failed American supersonic effort even less, Russia's Tu-144 was rushed ahead only partly as a propaganda exercise but as a failed attempt to provide a commercial competitor.

ABOVE: Soviet Premier Josef Stalin (front left) standing next to US President Harry S Truman at the Potsdam Conference in 1945, architects of the Cold War world. (US State Department)

This book explores all those facets of the Cold War and balances the propaganda of one side against the projected ideals of the other, showing misrepresentation of reality through the use of manipulated 'truth', and misinterpretation through the deliberate use of deception. Both sides in the ideological struggle for supremacy suffered from self-assurance, and only through the increasingly valuable connections across the political divide could the Cold War begin to wind down.

"This is a living prelude to current affairs, and it is on this premise that the story of that age is laid out."

More than half of today's global population were not alive when the Cold War ended and much detail about that period has already faded into the past. Yet the wars that define nations today and the legacy that new conflicts leave in a fractured world are as relevant to those who never lived through this period as to those who did.

The Cold War provided many lessons for the period that followed the collapse of the Soviet Union and a cynic could say that most have been lost or forgotten. Many of the players in this story are now dead, so cannot speak for themselves, but their testimony to a seismic change in world affairs brought about through those 45 years is as relevant today as it ever was. For this is a living prelude to current affairs, and it is on this premise that the story of that age is laid out over the following pages.

David Baker
Author

ABOVE: Divided by a double wall, the separation of Berlin into east and west sectors was representative of Cold War tensions around the world. (Neptuul-wikicommons)

CONTENTS

14

26

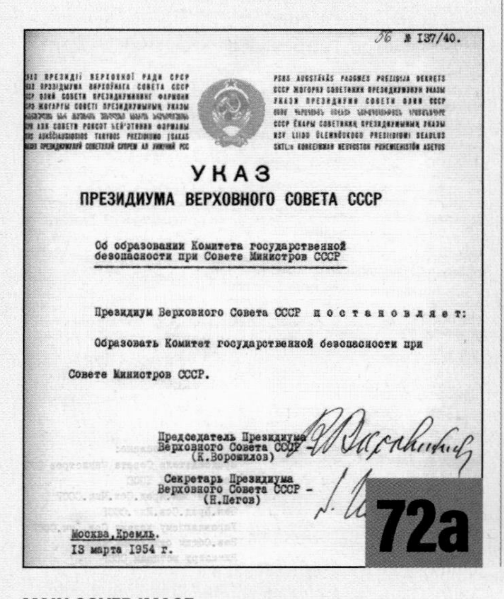

№ 137/40.

УКАЗ
ПРЕЗИДИУМА ВЕРХОВНОГО СОВЕТА СССР

Об образовании Комитета государственной безопасности при Совете Министров СССР

Президиум Верховного Совета СССР постановляет:

Образовать Комитет государственной безопасности при Совете Министров СССР.

Председатель Президиума Верховного Совета СССР - (К.Ворошилов)

Секретарь Президиума Верховного Совета СССР - (Н.Пегов)

Москва, Кремль.
13 марта 1954 г.

MAIN COVER IMAGE: (Daniren / Alamy Stock Photo)

ISBN: 978 1 80282 908 2
Editor: David Baker
Senior editor, specials: Roger Mortimer
Email: roger.mortimer@keypublishing.com
Cover design: Steve Donovan
Design: SJmagic DESIGN SERVICES, India
Advertising Sales Manager: Brodie Baxter
Email: brodie.baxter@keypublishing.com
Tel: 01780 755131
Advertising Production: Becky Antoniades
Email: rebecca.antoniades@keypublishing.com

SUBSCRIPTION/MAIL ORDER
Key Publishing Ltd, PO Box 300, Stamford, Lincs, PE9 1NA
Tel: 01780 480404
Subscriptions email: subs@keypublishing.com

Mail Order email: orders@keypublishing.com
Website: www.keypublishing.com/shop

PUBLISHING
Group CEO and Publisher: Adrian Cox
Published by
Key Publishing Ltd, PO Box 100, Stamford, Lincs, PE9 1XQ
Tel: 01780 755131 **Website:** www.keypublishing.com

PRINTING
Precision Colour Printing Ltd, Haldane, Halesfield 1, Telford, Shropshire. TF7 4QQ

DISTRIBUTION
Seymour Distribution Ltd, 2 Poultry Avenue, London, EC1A 9PU
Enquiries Line: 02074 294000.

A NEW WORLD ORDER

On February 4, 1945, leaders of the three then most powerful nations met to discuss the future of the world. For seven days they would discuss how the greatest conflict in history would end, how the victorious powers would determine the fate of conquered and suppressed countries, and how they would control the future of different political systems. National boundaries would be moved, great slices of subdued nations would be taken away and allocated to the victorious nations, and old scores would be settled.

Differences going back centuries would inform their decisions and the fate of several hundred million people would be decided through judgements made to favour the victors. The three countries meeting to make these decisions sent their leaders to the conference at Yalta, each of the delegations housed in three former Russian palaces in a beautiful part of the Crimean Peninsula on the northern shores of the Black Sea, Russia's southernmost coastal region.

For the United States, President Franklin D Roosevelt nursed ailing health and came sympathetic to the Soviet Union, suspicious of Britain's possible attempt to re-establish its empire in the Far East, which had been so savagely mauled by Imperial Japan. After lending support to Britain before it entered the war in December 1941, Roosevelt had found Britain's ideas of a post-war peace at variance with those of the United States. He died of a brain haemorrhage on April 12, 1945, two months after the Yalta conference. He was 63.

For the Russians, having suffered massive casualties from the greatest land battles in history, Premier Joseph Stalin came with demanding claims on control over East European countries he considered a threat to the post-war security of the Soviet Union. Stalin had old scores to settle with Poland, a historic enemy of Russia, and sought a corridor of connected buffer states from the Black Sea to the Baltic over which he could exert political control. He would die from a stroke at the Kuntsevo Dacha on March 5, 1953, at the age of 74.

For the British, Prime Minister Winston Churchill brought deep suspicions of communism and a determination to retain the semblance of Britain's global influence which even then he saw slipping from its grasp. Writer, correspondent, uniformed veteran of wars in Cuba, South Africa, India, and France, Churchill was an unashamed supporter of the British Empire, opponent of independence for British possessions, and a seasoned politician. He was Prime Minister from May 10, 1940, to July 26, 1945, and again from October 26, 1951, to April 5, 1955. He would die from the effects of a stroke on January 24, 1965, aged 90.

The Yalta Conference was set up at the behest of Roosevelt, who had wanted to get a three-power meeting to settle the post-war European situation before the November 7, 1944, US presidential election. On that day the incumbent beat James Dewey to a fourth session in the White House, the only president in US history to serve more than two consecutive terms. But the Yalta conference would be delayed. Several venues had been proposed but Stalin refused to travel far, claiming that his doctors advised against long journeys, but it was probably due more to his fear of flying. As the instigator, Roosevelt would play host and the critical meetings would be held at the Livadia Palace where the US delegation was housed.

From the outset, Stalin agreed that only a total and unconditional surrender of Germany would be acceptable. Surging west, Russian troops were already within striking distance of Berlin and the British and the Americans had pushed east, evicting Germany out of France and Belgium. There had been disagreement between members of the military leadership over the next moves, with several American generals urging Eisenhower to head for Berlin at full speed and beat the Soviets to the German

ABOVE: Allied leaders during World War Two gather for a summit at Yalta, February 4-11, 1945, to decide the fate of the post-war world. From left to right: British Prime Minister Winston Churchill, US President Franklin D Roosevelt, and Soviet Premier Josef Stalin. (NARA)

capital. But caution and the need for a sure victory with minimum Allied casualties prevented that.

When the Yalta conference convened the war was at a critical stage. On the defeat of Nazi Germany, there would be territories still occupied by its troops. After the German surrender, there would be a line in central Europe at which both British and American troops would come face to face with their Russian allies. For some, that was a difficult encounter to contemplate because the Russians had not always been allies of the western countries with which they had formed an alliance to defeat Nazi Germany. For almost two years they had been complicit in Hitler's crimes. The story of that would define the encroaching Cold War.

INTRIGUE AND CONSPIRACIES

In late August 1939, Russia had secretly negotiated a deal with Hitler to carve up Poland between them. Three weeks after Germany invaded Poland across its western border on September 1, 1939, Stalin attacked Poland from the east, eventually meeting German troops at an agreed point. The secret police of both invaders worked closely to purge Poland of political dissidents, Jews, gypsies, and opponents of the regime. But perhaps the alliance was not surprising, given the degree of secret

ABOVE: In August 1939, Stalin meets with Germany's Foreign Minister Franz von Ribbentrop to agree the combined attack on Poland, led by the Germans from the west on September 1 and by the Russians from the east on September 17. (Bundesarchiv)

cooperation between Germany and Russia after World War One.

Banned from possessing an independent armed force beyond certain restrictions imposed on Germany by the 1919 Treaty of Versailles, the newly created communist Russian Bolshevik state granted its former enemy access to training facilities for the development of a new German army and air force. All in secret and in contravention of the treaty. Long before Hitler brought his Nazi party to power in January 1933, the Russians had been training what would quickly emerge as well-prepared but still poorly equipped German armed services for land, sea, and air warfare.

Beginning in the early 1920s and from opposing sides of the political spectrum, Russian communists forged a deep connection with German military and political leaders in the then Weimar Republic to rebuild a new German state capable of assuaging what it felt to be the injustices of the 1919 peace agreement. The unlikely partnership had been mutually beneficial: Germany getting secret training facilities in return for a market through which it could sell heavy machinery as Stalin sought a massive industrialisation of his new Soviet state.

The danger was that the Russians were building up a powerful and resurgent Germany which could threaten it both politically and militarily. Stalin gambled on that threat because Russia had been frozen out of international banking systems by the overthrow of the imperialist Tsarist government together with its ruling class.

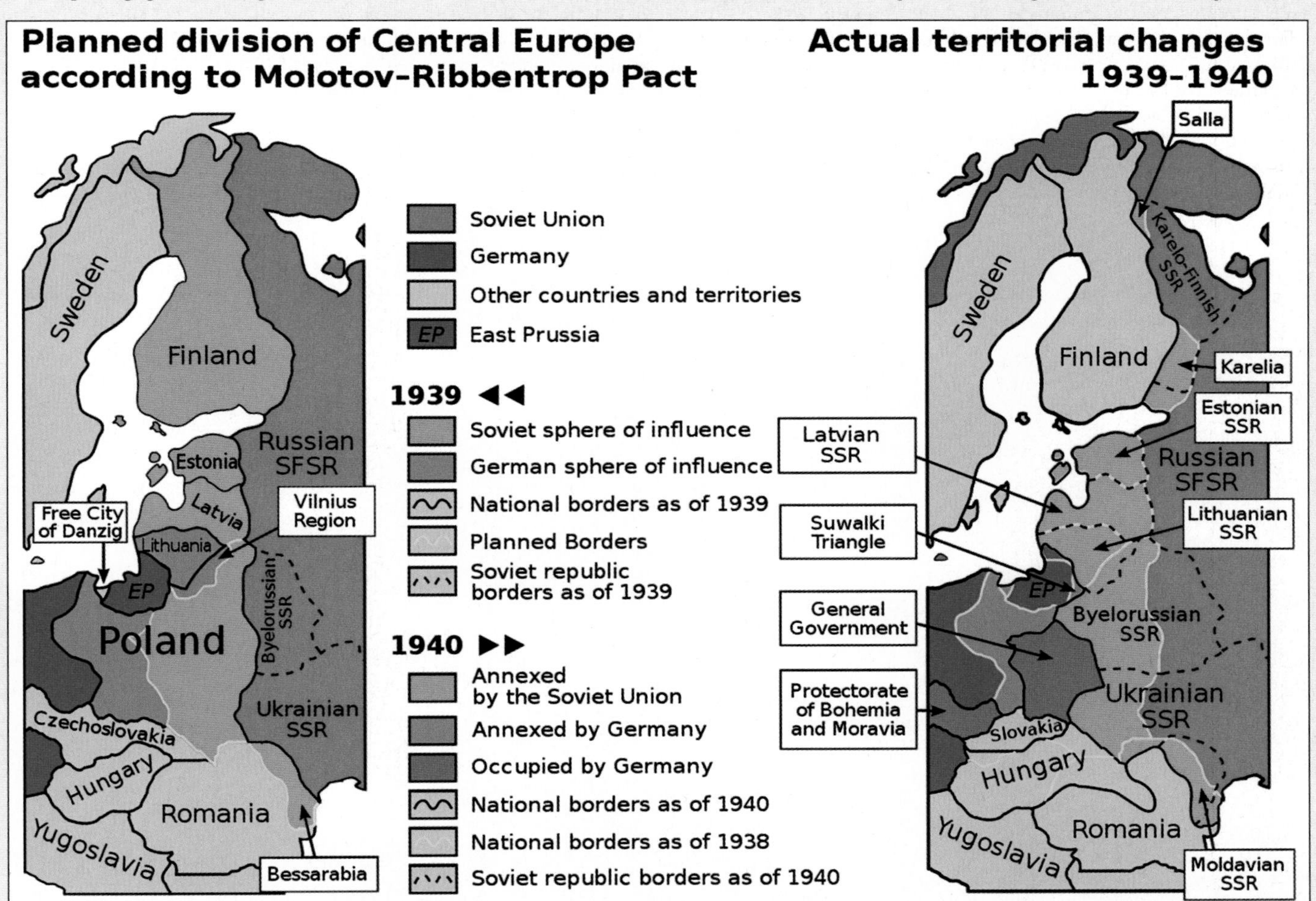

ABOVE: Having cooperated for several years, Germany and Russia planned a division of Europe into regions shared between the Nazis and the Soviets, as shown here where the planned changes shown on the left are compared with the actual changes which were achieved before Hitler attacked Russia in June 1941. (Peter Hanula)

It needed industrial material to convert Russia from a largely peasant society into a modern, highly industrialised and politically independent Soviet Union. But Stalin was playing with fire.

After he came to power in 1933, Hitler's anti-Soviet rhetoric and claims for German 'living-space' (lebensraum) in the east threatened to imbalance that relationship. For a brief period in the summer of 1939, Russian diplomats and some military commanders had negotiated secretly with the British through its embassy in Moscow for a pact whereby Hitler's ambitious land-grabs could be stopped by a pre-emptive strike against Germany. The Russians offered to put aside their historic enmity of the Poles and join forces with them and with the British to deliver an ultimatum to Hitler: Keep within your borders or suffer a military attack. It would require Britain to side with Stalin and oppose Germany before it could act.

Under the Russian plan, if Hitler did not desist from his territorial expansion, backed up by Poland and Britain they would declare war on Germany. The combined military might of the three countries would dramatically outnumber German forces. Moreover, said the Russians, they would have Germany in a pincer-grip, forces capable of attacking it from both sides. And they were quick to remind the British embassy diplomats that it had an empire to fall back on, adding further pressure on a belligerent Nazi Germany.

The British were horrified at the prospect of secretly plotting to declare war with Germany by aligning itself with the communist Russian state. British diplomats believed that negotiations alone could bring an end to Hitler's ambitions. The British had been political adversaries of the Soviet Union since the Bolshevik revolution and between 1918 and 1920 had sent troops to fight

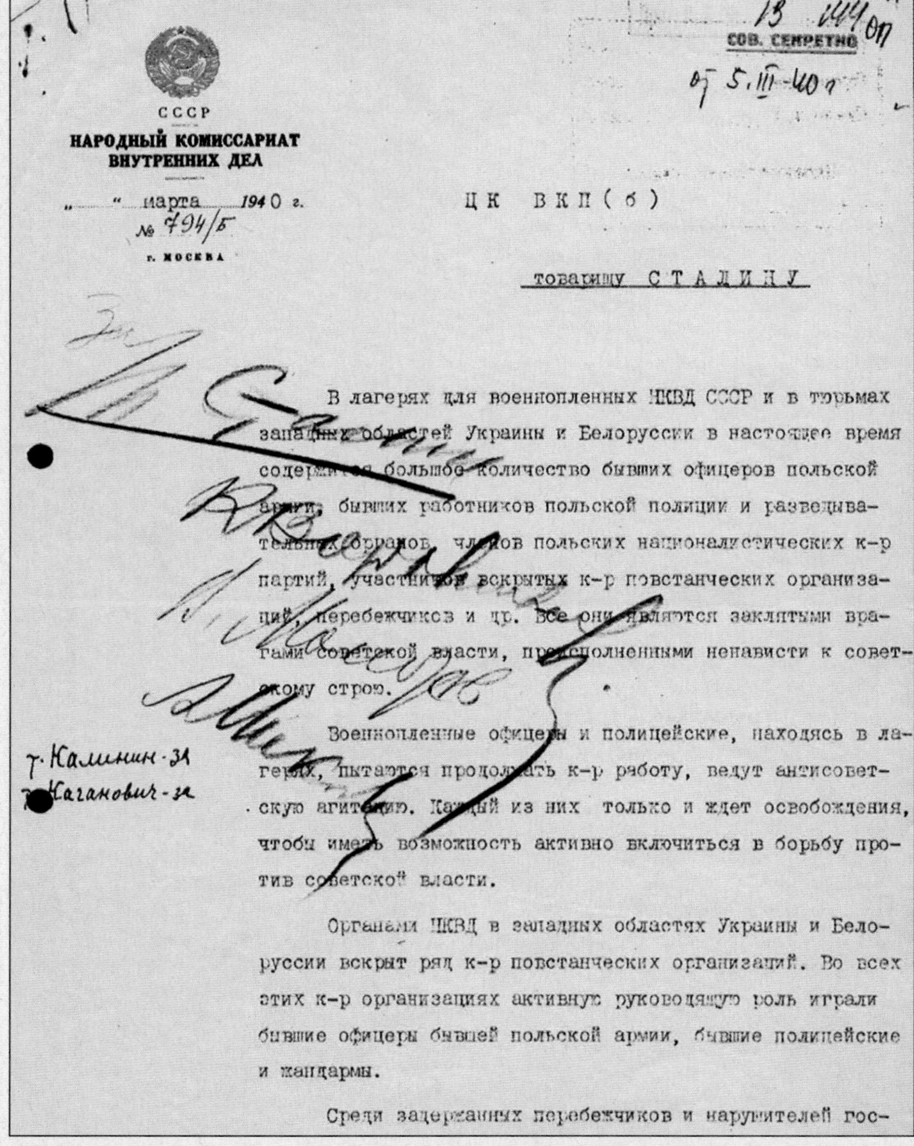

13 144/оп

СОВ. СЕКРЕТНО

от 5.III-40 г.

СССР

НАРОДНЫЙ КОМИССАРИАТ
ВНУТРЕННИХ ДЕЛ

„ “ марта 1940 г.
№ 794/Б

г. МОСКВА

ЦК ВКП(б)

товарищу СТАЛИНУ

В лагерях для военнопленных НКВД СССР и в тюрьмах западных областей Украины и Белоруссии в настоящее время содержится большое количество бывших офицеров польской армии, бывших работников польской полиции и разведывательных органов, членов польских националистических к-р партий, участников вскрытых к-р повстанческих организаций, перебежчиков и др. Все они являются заклятыми врагами советской власти, преисполненными ненависти к советскому строю.

Военнопленные офицеры и полицейские, находясь в лагерях, пытаются продолжать к-р работу, ведут антисоветскую агитацию. Каждый из них только и ждет освобождения, чтобы иметь возможность активно включиться в борьбу против советской власти.

Органами НКВД в западных областях Украины и Белоруссии вскрыт ряд к-р повстанческих организаций. Во всех этих к-р организациях активную руководящую роль играли бывшие офицеры бывшей польской армии, бывшие полицейские и жандармы.

Среди задержанных перебежчиков и нарушителей гос-

т. Калинин - за
т. Каганович - за

ABOVE: At the direction of the Communist Party of the Soviet Union, with this letter Stalin instructed Lavrentiy Beria, head of Russia's brutal secret police, to execute more than 20,000 Polish army officers, political leaders and those opposed to Marxist-Leninist doctrine. (RGASPI)

ABOVE: The Katowice-Pomnik memorial to the murdered Polish leadership, a crime which the Russians tried to blame on the Germans until forensic examination of the human remains proved otherwise. (Jan Mehlich)

on the side of White Russians struggling unsuccessfully to prevent the communists from taking over control of Russia and perhaps even its neighbouring countries.

There was another, underlying reason against the Russian offer. Why would the British wish to be implicit in starting a war against Germany using methods it had itself interpreted as a war crime over German mobilisation in 1914? But as the Russians pointed out, given their history they were unlikely to receive a friendly ear in Poland. It would need the British to take the Russian plan to the Polish government. After all, it had already given Poland reassurances that, if attacked, Britain would go to war to defend it against invasion.

The British embassy disregarded the plan as inappropriate and the embassy refused to pursue the matter with London, on the basis that it was outrageous. Nobody in the British government, least of all Prime Minister Chamberlain, wanted another world war. Moreover, after Chamberlain was rebuffed by France and by leaders in the British Commonwealth countries of Canada, India, Australia and New Zealand, the British government could not obtain their support to take a stronger and more militaristic tone with Hitler.

This had also been the dilemma over unilateral threats to Germany. Even the French, still reeling from the decimation of a generation in World War One, backed away from a threat of force should Germany choose territorial expansion. Consequently, negotiation was the sole remaining mechanism for opposing the Nazi regime while Britain re-armed at a higher rate of public investment than at any other time in its history, against the day that it would have to stand alone.

ABOVE: German women clearing rubble and shaving bricks for another use during the Allied occupation from 1945 to 1949. (Janczikowsky/wikicommons)

ABOVE: Political parties sprang up in West Germany after the war, this poster representing the Christian Democratic Union (CDU) carries the slogan "We cannot do magic – but we can do our job. Help us. Vote for CDU. It's about Germany". (Konrad-Adenauer Stiflung)

THE SEAL OF FATE

On learning of the British embassy refusal to discuss a tripartite ultimatum to Germany, on August 23, 1939, Stalin's foreign minister Vyacheslav Molotov signed the secret deal with his German equivalent, Joachim von Ribbentrop. This allowed the Germans to invade Poland and to join the land grab by taking over the Baltic states and by attacking Finland in an attempt to extend the borders of the Soviet Union to Norway and Sweden. All with the agreement of the Germans, but with consequences far beyond those expected.

Russia had been a major trading partner with the Germans since the middle of the 19th century. Anticipating the inevitable resurgence of a new Germany after the war, in 1920 Russia had secretly made known its wish for occupying substantial areas of what was then Poland, a common enemy of both countries. It encouraged Germany to think of a single solution to the Polish problem which had haunted the foreign policies of both countries for several centuries. When the Russians invaded on September 17, 1939, Soviet secret police and army units seized and executed 22,000 people judged to be 'counter-revolutionaries' together with the government and military leadership in a genocide subsequently known as the Katyn massacre.

In November 1939, Stalin invaded Finland and the British pledged arms which were in fact short on delivery due to an urgent need to build up its own forces for an anticipated attack on the UK by Germany. Britain had not declared war on Russia when it invaded Poland, but this was the first occasion in which it came close to doing so. Although, in effect, Russia was as much an enemy of Britain due to its unprovoked invasion of Poland. Throughout the war, academics and historians debated why this was so, although many concluded that following a declaration of war against Germany with a declaration of war with Russia several weeks later was tantamount to bringing down the whole world on its head!

There was, however, an equally pragmatic reason. Unknown to the general public, the defence agreement pledging Britain's support for Poland specifically defined an attack by Germany and named no other country. Britain had no legal obligation to do so but the matter brought rumblings of discontent throughout Parliament, while concern was rife over the fate of Finland, struggling successfully to hold off the Soviet army against all its best efforts. So it was that when the Polish ambassador Edward Raczyński asked Lord Halifax, the British foreign secretary for help, it was refused.

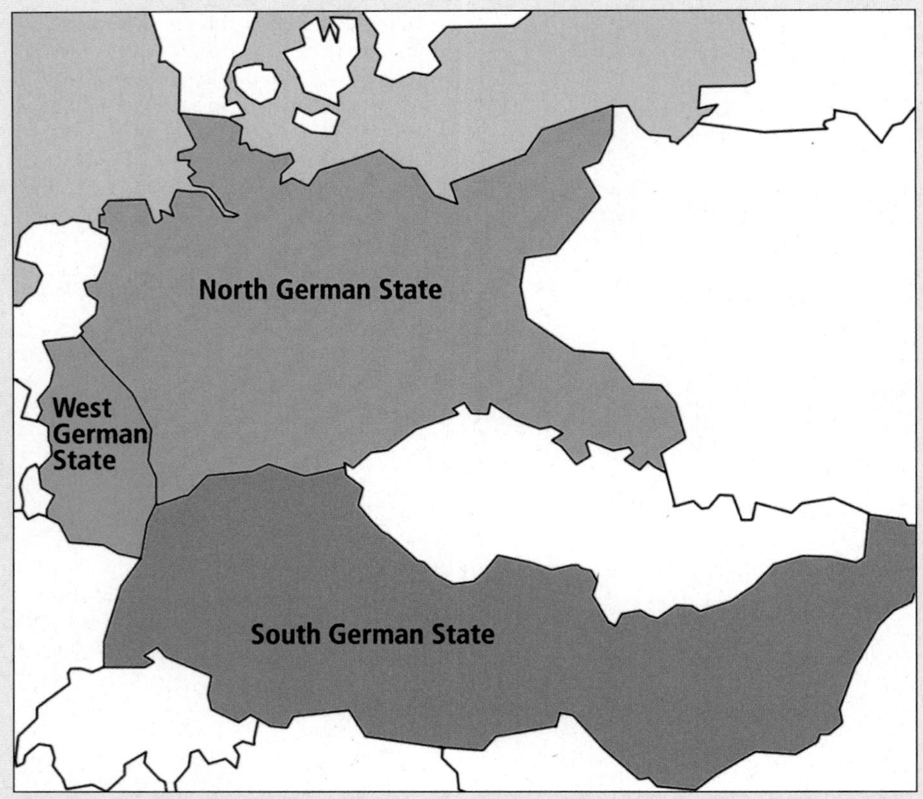

ABOVE: Under the partition plan proposed by Winston Churchill, West Germany would be divided into three separate zones with the South German State also including Austria and Hungary. (Domie – commonswiki)

While German forces overran France and the Low Countries on May 10, 1940, believing the world to be preoccupied with the lightning blitzkrieg, Soviet troops prepared to surge into the Baltic states and did so during June. Government officials were replaced by Soviet substitutes which would eventually lead to the execution of 170,000 people as Russia tightened its grip, seeding hatred among the populations of Latvia, Estonia, and Lithuania.

For a time, it seemed Russia was on the winning side. On September 27, 1940, Germany, Italy, and Japan signed its own tripartite, this bond of the Axis powers acting as a deterrent to interference from the United States. The pivotal moment for Russia came on June 22, 1941, when the largest land invasion in history unleashed more than three million German troops and several thousand aircraft in a lightning attack on the Soviet Union. It was waged across a front eventually extending from the Gulf of Finland to the Black Sea.

Not completely unexpected by the Russians, it came with great ferocity and with the purpose of clearing vast swathes of land for German settlement and the use of local peasants for slave labour. As had been the practice in Poland, ethnic cleansing became an integral part of the invasion, which had been given the name Barbarossa after the 12th century Holy Roman Emperor who gave Germany predominance in Europe. Within a week more than 30 Soviet divisions had been destroyed and the German army was within 300 miles (480km) of Moscow.

Immediately after Hitler attacked the Soviet Union the Russians had appealed to Britain and America for help. But that required an unexpected reversal of position and there was confusion about the consequences due to heavy and mutual suspicion of each other's intentions. Britain conferred with its Commonwealth allies and on July 12, 1941, Sir Stafford Cripps, the British ambassador in Moscow, signed an agreement with Molotov binding the two countries as allies against Germany. Churchill was at pains to point out that this was an alliance between the people of Britain and the people of Russia and not an endorsement of the Soviet Union and its political ideologies.

As the alliance progressed and Russia received vast quantities of aid in the form of armaments and munitions, further discussions resulted in a second agreement, signed by the then British Foreign Secretary Anthony Eden and Molotov on May 26, 1942. In it, both parties agreed to remain allies until the end of the war and for 20 years thereafter. There had been no consultation with the Commonwealth or the United States and neither Churchill nor Stalin defined precisely what it meant. It was, however, clear that after the war Russia would want to retain the Baltic states and Finland which it had obtained under its pact with Hitler.

For the next three years, Britain, the United States, and the Soviet Union fought a slogging land and air campaign against the dwindling capabilities of Nazi Germany. As the end neared there were concerns that a new world order would be set by decisions made at the Yalta conference. It was the last time the three world leaders met together and the fate of the world would hang in the balance dependent entirely upon how their successors would struggle to keep the peace

THE BIG DECISIONS

Not everyone who thought they should be there were present at the Yalta conference. France had not been invited and that would cause bitter resentment from its leader, Gen de Gaulle who had maintained a Free French government in waiting from war-torn London. De Gaulle fled France after the German invasion of May 10, 1940, and surrender terms which put Marshal Philippe Pétain as leader of the Vichy government under overall German authority of the southern part of the country.

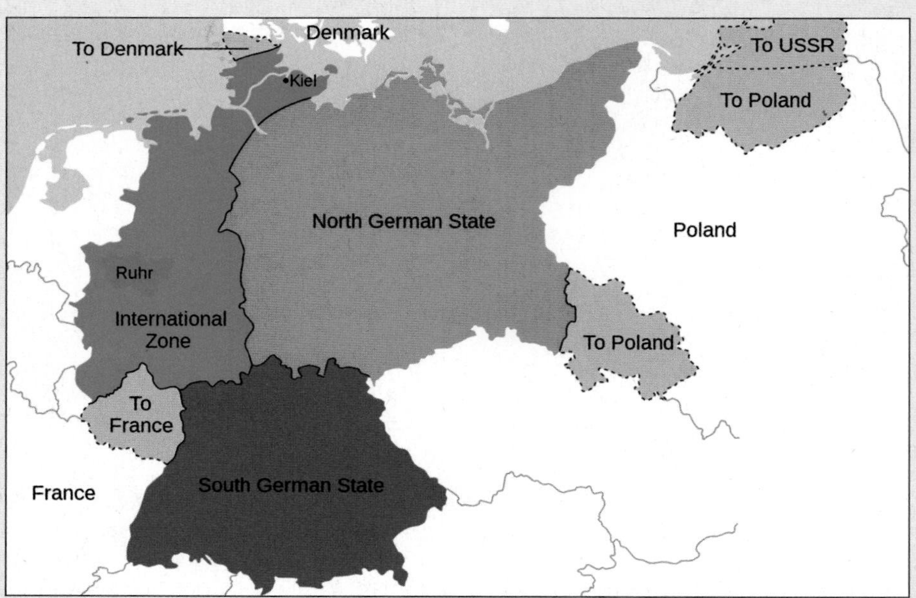

ABOVE: Henry Morgenthau proposed a Germany with a similar division to that imagined by Churchill with geographic territory given to Poland and Russia. Denmark would inherit a part of Schleswig-Holstein. (Erinthecute/wikicommons)

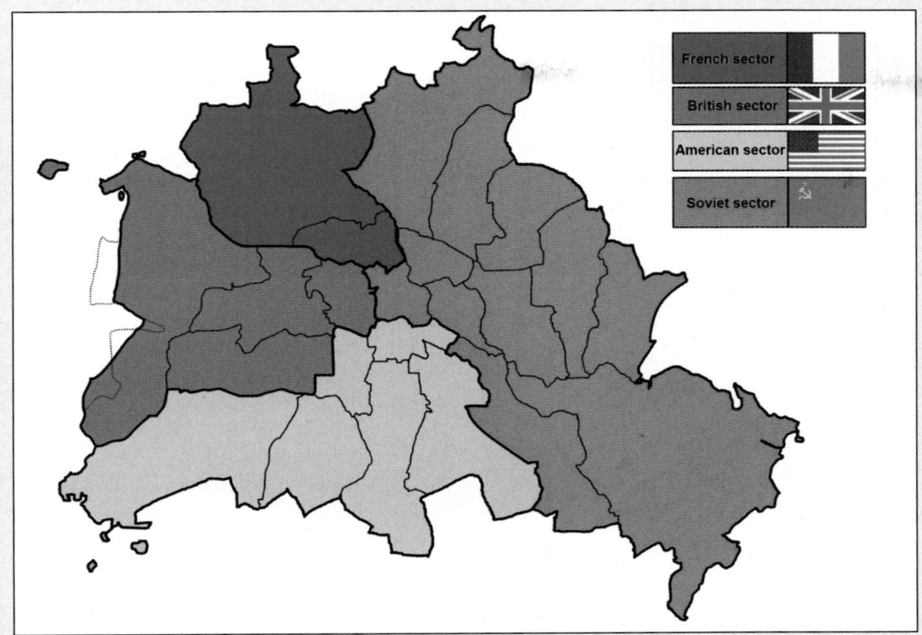

ABOVE: By agreement among the Allies, Berlin was divided into sectors controlled by the Soviet Union, the United States, Britain, and France, as identified here by national flags. (Paasikivi/Wikicommons)

ABOVE: Prime Minister Winston Churchill (foreground) receives a commemorative photograph of the opening days of the Potsdam conference from President Harry Truman, watched over by Harold Macmillan as Dean Acheson (background) consults his notes. (NARA)

It had been a disturbing time for Britain, effectively at war with Vichy France as it operated under rules dictated from Berlin, until November 1942 when Germany took total control of that region after the allies landed in North Africa and threatened France's Mediterranean coast. Churchill had ordered the destruction of much of the French naval fleet at Mers-el-Kebir in French Algeria on July 3, 1940, shortly after France capitulated, neutralising it as a potential German asset, albeit at the cost of 1,297 killed and 350 wounded.

Poland was the most important priority for Russia at the Yalta conference, and this became the focus for much of the discussions over post-war Europe. Stalin was determined to retain territory seized under cooperation with Nazi Germany and would agree that Poland's western border should be relocated west of its pre-war line at the expense of post-war Germany. Opposed to the Polish government-in-waiting in London, Stalin had already set in motion arrangements for the country's leadership by purging pro-democratic politicians as the Red Army swept German troops out of Poland and began a process of installing pro-Russian officials.

All were agreed that nothing short of the total and unconditional surrender of Germany was acceptable but the way it would be governed was open to controversy. The economist and secretary of the US treasury, Henry Morgenthau submitted a plan to government advocating that Germany should be permanently disarmed, that Poland should acquire large tracts of East Prussia and that the industrial Ruhr should be governed by an international consortium and that other areas should be divided up into a North German State and a South German State.

In discussions over this plan, Morgenthau wanted to prevent Germany from ever again being able to produce any industrial activity and that the population should be held at a subsistence level governed by other European countries. Churchill was opposed to the idea, telling Roosevelt that if it was implemented "England would be chained to a dead body." When the plan was analysed in detail it implied that 40% of the population would die and the remainder be left to their own resources, living off the land.

Roosevelt discussed the matter further with Lord Cherwell, Churchill's science adviser, who agreed with the President and took the matter further to the Prime Minister. Churchill was left in no doubt that approval for $6.5bn in post-war credits would require Roosevelt's agreement, which was sufficient to change his mind. A staunch opponent of the Morgenthau plan, Anthony Eden persuaded the British government to think again while Roosevelt claimed that he was only thinking of Britain by suggesting they have a slice of industries in the Ruhr. When examining it in detail, Roosevelt recoiled, asserting that it was "wise to abandon any *final solution*" – at the very least, a poor choice of words.

The final determination over Europe was that it would be divided into four sectors under Russian, British, American and French governance, as would Berlin which would be in the eastern sector under the control of the Russians. At the very least, Germany would be subject to a thorough denazification process to purge it ideologically and culturally of its associations with the Hitler regime. In reality, this would only be partly achieved, several thousand German bureaucrats and former government officials being used to conduct the day-to-day work

ABOVE: When the 'Big Three' met at Potsdam to finalise decisions on post-war Europe, newly elected British Prime Minister Clement Attlee (left) replaced Winston Churchill and had his first encounter with Josef Stalin (right) and Harry S Truman. (NARA)

of restoring to the country's citizens some semblance of a normal existence.

Distrust was rife at Yalta. Stalin was already suspicious of British duplicity, having been informed that it had discussed with senior German generals the possibility of an early surrender, taking the heat of battle out of certain sectors as the war ground to a stop. Not directly connected to the Yalta conference, it is an example of how the Russians had penetrated British and American planning sessions. When confronted with this, Churchill was aghast and sent a suitably incensed reply: "I cannot avoid a feeling of bitter resentment towards your informers, whoever they are, for such vile misrepresentations of my actions or those of my trusted subordinates."

There were grounds for distrust, however. Highly suspicious of Stalin's plan for Poland, and his assertion that he would support democratic free choice for its people, Churchill instigated a secret plan to prepare for a pre-emptive strike on the Soviet Union to support Polish freedoms. Code named 'Operation Unthinkable', it projected that the Russians would maintain a powerful standing army in Eastern Europe and that it could impose its will at random unless threatened with unstoppable force. One of the reasons for this was "to impose upon Russia the will of the United States and the British Empire".

Churchill was aware that if the atomic bomb performed as described – it had yet to be tested – it would place in the hands of the West a weapon of such devastating potential that it could overturn all the conventions of war. The military response was to dissuade Churchill from any further planning, on the basis that the Russian army would be so powerful that it would be impossible for Britain to win any such conflict. A further request from Churchill sought guidance on the requirements necessary to "ensure the security of the British Isles in the event of war with Russia in the near future".

Even as the existing war in Europe was winding up, Churchill was concerned that the mass movement of American forces from Britain to the war against Japan would leave the country vulnerable and exposed to a sudden assault from Russian forces. In the event, Japan surrendered before any invasion was necessary and demobilisation took American troops from the UK and not to another war front. Consistent throughout the Yalta talks was a palpable sense of distrust with all parties engaged in evasive diplomatic language and outright obfuscation.

Before the surrender of Japan, a final conference was held in Potsdam outside Berlin and after the Germans had surrendered. It had been delayed by Truman until after the atomic bomb had been tested at Alamogordo, New Mexico and just prior to its use on the Japanese cities of Hiroshima and Nagasaki. The conference opened on July 17, 1945, at which Roosevelt's successor Harry S Truman and Churchill were present, accompanied by their foreign ministers and a large number of diplomats and senior advisers, joined a day later by Stalin.

The mood was sour from the outset and distrust between the Western leaders and the Soviet Union was at a new height. Since Yalta and the end of the war in Europe, Stalin had taken full control of Eastern Europe, pulled the Baltic states into the Soviet sphere without the promised elections and taken an assertive role across East Germany. The Russians were revelling in their new-found role as a victorious occupying force. Unlike Roosevelt, Truman was critical of Stalin and aware that Germany would need help to build a new, democratic society and that other European countries would require financial assistance to rebuild their own economies.

Midway through the Potsdam conference, Churchill left to fight a general election and lost to Labour's Clement Attlee, who replaced

ABOVE: The Potsdam Conference defined borders decided for post-war European countries with Russia acquiring buffer states to absorb the first assault on any war between the USSR and Western countries, this diagram showing border changes since 1938. (Author's collection)

him for the final series of talks before it wound up on August 2, 1945. The division of Germany and Berlin agreed at Yalta was endorsed, as was the complete denazification of Germany with territories seized during the war returned and the border with Poland shifted westward on a line from Stettin on the Baltic south along the rivers Oder and Neisse. This reduced the area of Germany by one-quarter to its size in 1937 and just over one-third from its borders before World War One. Further to that, a wide range of reparations were to be paid by Germany with a limit on German national income to no more than the European average.

DEMOBILISATION

After six years of war, the British servicemen and women were sent back to civilian life but at a pace that brought frustration and complaints. Nevertheless, by 1947 about 4.3m had been 'demobbed' but not fast enough for war-weary veterans in far-flung places and civilians exhausted from the 'blitz' at home in the UK. And around the world in Commonwealth countries, Allied forces re-joined their communities. National shortages of food, housing and money and clothing added to the social consequences of men who had been away from their families for several years. In 1947 the divorce rate was at an all-time high with more than 60,000 applications compared with just over 8,000 in 1939, a figure which would not be exceeded before the early 1970s when new liberal reform laws were introduced.

In the United States, by July 1947, eight million uniformed soldiers had been returned to civilian life, leaving about 684,000 men in military service. This reduction was driven by the frugal budget plans of President Truman, who believed that demobilisation was a key to post-war economic success. There was a belief that the strategic bomber would be sufficient deterrent to any potential aggressor and that it would be unnecessarily expensive to retain a large standing army. In the United States, rapid conversion to a domestic consumer economy would not come as quickly as many economists believed and pressure to provide financial assistance to war-torn Europe became an unexpected burden on the federal budget.

ABOVE: During the ceremony for the formal surrender of the Japanese on September 2, 1945, the US Navy conducted a mass fly-by of 450 aircraft from the Third Fleet, seen by sailors on the more than 300 ships from many different nations in Tokyo Bay. (NARA)

Contrary to repeated assertions in many publications, up to the present, the Soviet Union quickly demobilised after the war, reducing its armed services from 11.3m men and women to approximately 2.8m by 1948, with combat troops making up 85% of that total. A considerable reshaping of the armed services came after the war, Stalin exhibiting a fear bordering on paranoia that the Western allies would organise an attack on the Soviet Union. Consolidated Russian land forces maintained a strong presence in Eastern Europe as the Soviet Union strengthened its grip on political administration and military managements of their internal affairs.

As the war ended when Japan surrendered in September 1945, the scene was set for heightened tension between countries that collectively sacrificed a generation to defeat Nazi Germany and Imperial Japan. On March 5, 1946, Winston Churchill gave a speech to an audience at Fulton, Missouri, on the impending challenges for democracies everywhere. After an introduction from President Harry Truman, a part of this address announced the beginning of a new struggle, a Cold War against which Churchill projected grave foreboding:

"From Stettin in the Baltic to Trieste in the Adriatic, an iron curtain has descended across the Continent. Behind that line lie all the capitals of the ancient states of Central and Eastern Europe. Warsaw, Berlin, Prague, Vienna, Budapest, Belgrade, Bucharest and Sofia, all these famous cities and the populations around them lie in what I must call the Soviet sphere...

"Athens alone – Greece with its immortal glories – is free to decide its future at an election under British, American and French observation. The Russian-dominated Polish government has been encouraged to make enormous and wrongful inroads upon Germany, and mass expulsions of millions of Germans on a scale grievous and undreamed-of are now taking place.

"The safety of the world requires a new unity in Europe, from which no nation should be permanently outcast…Surely we should work with conscious purpose for a grand pacification of Europe, within the structure of the United Nations and in accordance with our Charter. That I feel is an open cause of policy of very great importance."

Churchill's 'iron curtain' speech defined the end of an era and the beginning of a new age, one in which two superpower states would preside over the demise of empires and fight through conflict, proxy wars, propaganda and a struggle for supremacy in a Cold War which would last 45 years and reshape forever the future beyond that.

ABOVE: Presided over by General Douglas MacArthur, the Japanese surrender is signed on the deck of the battleship USS *Missouri*. (NARA)

A FIGHT FOR SURVIVAL

For different reasons, to each of the victorious powers Germany was the central focus of attention at the Yalta and Potsdam conferences. It was there that the division of Germany and of Berlin was ratified by Russia, the United States, Britain, and France. The geographic areas assigned to each country were largely, but not directly, prescribed by the area their forces occupied at the time of the surrender, apart from the westward migration of the border with Poland. Overall administrative management of Germany would be under the Allied Control Council, a body formed to govern the country but not as two separate spheres of political influence which it would quickly become.

It had not been the intention of the victorious powers that Germany would be divided but that would quickly become the case as Soviet intentions became more apparent. The Allied Control Council had conferred with a consultative body known as the European Advisory Commission, set up in October 1943 as a channel between the foreign ministries of Russia, the USA and Britain. Based in Lancaster House, London, from January 14, 1944, the following year France was admitted too. Recommending post-war political restructuring of Europe, it placed governance within the four separate occupying powers and not through the Allied Control Council. In doing so, it opened the opportunity for Moscow to treat its East European zone as it wished and without further consultation.

Many politicians would come to see this as a grave error, giving Russia carte blanche over how it treated East European countries, increasingly heavy-handed and determined to impose its political ideology and prevent democratic elections. Set up at the Potsdam Conference, the Council of Foreign Minsters established conditions for peace treaties with Italy, Romania, Bulgaria, and Finland. After the invasion of Russia by Germany in June 1941, Finland became an ally of Germany because it had assisted the Finns to throw out the Russian invaders. Because of that it was considered an ally of the former Nazi state and, despite suffering grievously at the hands of the Russians, was considered to be an 'enemy', but only in the literal sense.

The Council of Foreign Ministers superseded the European Advisory Commission, a body that had played a vital role in addressing the problems of Europe as those of the continent which it considered as a single entity and not as a group of separate countries which previously had been competitively and militarily independent of each other. It was not the first body to propose a pan-European zone of cooperation and it would be some time before that concept would emerge from political groups campaigning for a body to represent the interests of the continent rather than to engage in wasteful competitiveness. But it was the formative origin of the European Union.

In the minds of some political thinkers, the rise of the United States as the world's major economic power several decades earlier at the expense of the British Empire provided a good reason for abandoning national competition for a united competitiveness with the new trading power. Thus was the European Advisory Commission a meeting ground for different ideological factions, supported by communists who envisaged a united world run by state operatives as well as by free-market democrats who imagined a world in which collective cooperation between countries could proceed disconnected from big government. But there was another body uniting many nations, both inside and outside the European continent.

BELOW: The headquarters building of the Allied Control Council in Schönenberg, set up in 1945 to administrate post-war Germany. (Bruhaha on de Wikipedia)

"From October 1, 1947, when China's communist party seized control of the country, two members of the council were ideological adversaries of free Western democracies."

ABOVE: Three weeks after the Russian attack on Russia and four months before Japan attacked Pearl Harbor, President Roosevelt (left) meets with Prime Minister Churchill for a Sunday service on the deck of the HMS *Prince of Wales* at an Atlantic conference on August 10, 1941. Standing at the extreme right is General George C Marshall and Admiral E J King of the US Navy. (Imperial War Museum)

On September 24, 1941, a London meeting of the eight governments in exile under Axis occupation together with the Soviet Union and the Free French, agreed to principles outlined by Britain and the US which would govern the post-war world to ensure peace. These had been laid down at a meeting three months previously at which a wider range of nations had pledged their support for what would emerge as the United Nations (UN). The principles and protocols were taken directly from what would become known as the Atlantic Charter, so coined by the *Daily Herald*, a newspaper sympathetic to the Labour Party. Signed by Roosevelt and Churchill on August 14, 1941, aboard the HMS *Prince of Wales*, it embodied aspirations for the world after the defeat of Nazi Germany and Imperial Japan and would inspire the Declaration of the United Nations signed on January 1, 1942.

The first meeting of the UN took place in San Francisco, California, on April 25, 1945, two weeks before the final surrender of Germany. Fifty countries attended and the UN formally came into existence on October 24, 1945, a month after the signing of the Japanese surrender and upon ratification by the US, Britain, France, the Soviet Union, and China, the five permanent members of the Security Council. But there would be difficulties as the political differences between member states began to dictate attitudes within the General Assembly.

The United Nations had no separate powers of enforcement and no ability to intervene militarily except through the recruited services of independent countries. From October 1, 1947, when China's communist party seized control of the country, two members of the council were ideological adversaries of free Western democracies, a factor which would haunt the UN for several decades as it fought to maintain its articles of association.

A DIVIDED GERMANY

The way Germany was divided by political affiliation after World War Two was in keeping with the struggle between the Left and the Right in the period after the previous global war. A civil war had raged in Germany between 1918 and 1919 where communist revolutionaries sowed seeds of discontent among the soldiers and sailors of the Imperial Germany, fomenting a revolution and sponsoring widespread mutiny. Large numbers of German troops laid down their arms and walked back home while others had shot their officers and gone on the run.

As Germany appealed for an armistice and the Kaiser Wilhelm II fled to the Netherlands in exile, a fractious pause was instigated behind the scenes by US President Woodrow Wilson's roving diplomat and personal adviser Edward M House. Faced with an ultimatum, the British and the French were forced to follow the American plan and the armistice was formalised.

But the conflict between political extremist philosophies raged on, and in the run up to Hitler coming to power in January 1933, street battles and beer-hall brawls led to fierce fist-fights between opposing political factions. After 1933, the communists and those opposed to the Nazi regime were removed, either to concentration camps or the gallows. Yet, despite the brutal and inhuman suppression of free thought, the beliefs and political affiliations of left-wing and communist supporters never went away and would re-emerge 12 years later.

As World War Two drew to a close in 1945, people began to talk more openly and to form small groups, supported by infiltrators sent from Moscow to gather support for extreme forms of socialism and for the establishment of a communist state. In government factories and research

ABOVE: Widow of the former president, Eleanor Roosevelt reads the Declaration of Human Rights underpinning a charter of 'universal truths' established by the United Nations. (FDR Presidential Library & Museum)

ABOVE: In addition to dealing with political tensions between East and West, British and American occupation forces administered 23 'Rhine Meadows' prisoner-of-war camps through which three million German military personnel were processed for release or incarceration. France received 180,000 for forced labour. (Maximilian Dorrbecker)

establishments, small groups of intellectuals, academics, managers, workers, and artisans grouped into cells which anticipated a post-fascist world in which people could once again live free and uninterrupted by fear – but in a state run by the state and not for the people, the individual subservient to the benefit of the masses, as determined by a non-elected group of overlords.

At the very end of the war, groups of these left-wing thinkers set off for the Russian lines and were welcomed into what would become Eastern Europe, while others, finding themselves trapped, took every opportunity to flee to the West. Framed from the Communist Party of Germany, which had existed since World War One, gathering together anti-war groups as well as those wanting a hard-left socialist government. Because the struggle between Left and Right in political thought had been most strongly fought out in Germany, after World War Two it was inevitable that these groups would again become dominant.

During mid-1945, in the Russian zone of what had become East Germany, Stalin unified these different groups and formed the Socialist Unity Party (SED). Officials from Moscow moved in and lobbied among the people for support of a democratic regime which, they assured the people, would have no connection with Marxist-Leninist theory. It was a lie. As machinery, technicians, engineers, research facilities and technical innovations developed in Hitler's Germany were lifted and taken to the Soviet Union, the military forbad the formation of any other political group. While honouring free elections, in reality the only people

ABOVE: German prisoners were rounded up from across Germany and their service records examined to identify wanted criminals for genocide or war crimes. (US Army)

standing as candidates were officials from the communist party. This ensured that those elected were true to Moscow's political ideology but also directly approved of by the population, which ensured compliance.

Buoyed by his success at Yalta and Potsdam in getting agreement for the partitioning of Europe, in 1946 Stalin circulated to visiting leaders of communist Bulgaria and Yugoslavia that soon the whole of Germany would have to be brought together under a communist flag and absorbed into the Soviet Union. He said he was convinced that through subversive undermining of support for the British and the Americans they could be ousted from West Berlin and from their respective sectors in West Germany, clearing the way for all of Germany to be absorbed into the Soviet bloc before persuasive elements in Italy, France, and the Low Countries repeated the process there.

ABOVE: In the holding facilities at the 'Rhine Meadows' camps, conditions were dire, food was scarce and there were frequent episodes of retribution as British and US soldiers liberated death camps and saw for themselves the indescribable horrors perpetrated by the Nazis. (US Army)

DYSFUNCTIONAL NEIGHBOURS

Where once, under Roosevelt and initially Truman, the Americans had wanted to keep Germany impoverished, unindustrialised and unable to rise again with militaristic ambitions, by 1946 Truman had reversed his opinion. On pragmatic grounds of not wanting to open the door to communists and because of the need to help Germany become a self-supporting country without burdening the other countries of Western Europe, the mood changed dramatically.

Ways would have to be sought to give Germans a renewed sense of purpose rather than impoverishment, a mechanism found for improving their lives and rebuilding a democratic society.

Under reparations agreed at Potsdam, West German industrial resources were to be sent to Russia but when the East German guards stopped reciprocal supplies

> "The first meeting of the UN took place in San Francisco, California, on April 25, 1945, two weeks before the final surrender of Germany."

ABOVE: The vast programme of rebuilding Germany and its economy was assisted by the Marshall Plan of foreign aid provided by the United States, displayed here on a poster to encourage a population hungry for reconstitution. (St Krekeler on de Wikipedia)

of agricultural products, the US commander General Lucius D Clay stopped shipments of machinery from the West. This triggered a disruptive Soviet policy of upsetting administrative interactions between the four powers and slowed the movement of goods. The Americans were increasingly moving toward a policy of establishing a self-governing West German state by 1949 but at local elections on October 20, 1946, for 130 members of the Berlin City Council across all four sectors, the population of East Berlin delivered a massive anti-communist protest vote.

Impressed with the resourcefulness of the German people, the American government was more determined than ever that the burden of reconstitution should not fall on the rest of Europe but be paid for by the Germans themselves, a people who had voted very high in election polls to keep Hitler in power. As a starting point, on January 1, 1947, the British and the Americans joined forces to combine their zones into a unified economic sector, a fundamental first step toward independence and the re-establishment of a West German currency.

Continuing their campaign of disruption and intervention, the Russians began to

> **"While it would be some time before the Russians could attack the continental United States, all of Europe was within range of conventional aircraft carrying atomic weapons."**

expansion were denied when the Japanese defeated the Czar's forces in the 1904-1905 war. In repressive occupation and defeated by a violent and obsessive campaign to control Korea, Japan imposed harsh rule. When Japan attacked China in 1937 it conscripted several tens of thousands of Korean men, and 200,000 girls and women were forced into sexual slavery for Japanese soldiers throughout the war.

With no independent government, or a representative body of political affiliation for the post-war peace, at a conference in Cairo in 1943 the allied powers endorsed a plan whereby the northern part of the country would be administered by the Soviet Union and the southern half by the United States. The border was defined by a line of latitude 38° north of the equator – the 38th parallel – endorsed by the UN and without any real consideration of the indigenous people, albeit with strenuous objections from the Soviet Union.

Initially, life under the Soviets was less controlled than those of the East European states. Although it had entered the capital Pyongyang as early as August 24, 1945, Russian soldiers made only slow progress with identifying Marxist sympathisers. Until Moscow exercised stricter controls on the behaviour of its troops, Korea suffered the same abusive treatment and bandit-behaviour as had many citizens of Eastern Europe under Russian occupation.

From spring 1946 the Russians began to impose land reforms of the type that had been so disastrous in Russia and the Ukraine during the 1930s, general conditions and the treatment of civilians being so harsh that over the year around 400,000 North Koreans migrated to South Korea. Under Japanese rule, most of the country's industry had been concentrated in the north, leaving farming and agriculture in the southern lands where its people could carry out more traditional practices supporting their largely agrarian lifestyle.

With a bilateral agreement that the ruling parties would withdraw after elections, voters in the South went to the polls on May 10, 1948, with Syngman Rhee elected as president. Voters in the North cast their ballot on August 15 and the Russians agreed to install Kim Il Sung to lead a communist government. Stalin saw his opportunity and the Kremlin worked with Kim to prepare for an invasion of South Korea. The UN urged Russia and America to vacate their positions but to support these now independent states in their respective sectors. Moscow withdrew its forces on December 10, 1948, followed by the Americans a year later.

PREPARATIONS FOR WAR

Over the following 18 months the North became increasingly aggressive, ignoring the right of the UN to agree to the previous division at the 38th parallel as it sent guerrilla raids into the South to foment conflict at a local level. Kim threatened the South militarily and directed his vitriol at the UN, which he claimed he would drive out of Korea completely, unite the country and establish a communist regime throughout the entire peninsula. Inspired by a so far silent partner, Kim sought help from Russia and secret deals were reached over the supply of arms.

ABOVE: Chiang Kai-shek succeeded Sun Yat-sen and fought against the rising popularity of the communist party led by Mao Zedong but the two joined forces to fight the Japanese invaders. Here, Generalissimo and Madame Chiang Kai-shek share a joke with Lieutenant General Joseph W Stilwell commanding the China Expeditionary Forces. (US DoD)

It suited Moscow's world view that after its own march west into large swathes of Eastern Europe, and with China encompassing a quarter of the world's population and now a fellow member of the communist club, it should want to see the whole of Korea come under Marxist-Leninist doctrine. Stalin saw himself in no less a position than Hitler had sought when bringing Italy and Japan into his 'Pact of Steel' but reimagined into a tripartite alliance of communist states. There were risks in this, but the atomic bomb had given Stalin political, if not yet military, confidence while, for the moment, he played the role of silent partner, a paranoid fear of American military capabilities.

Not everyone in South Korea supported the installed government of Syngman Rhee though. Beginning shortly after the elections, in late 1948 socialist groups in South Korea carried out local uprisings with defectors from the South Korean army attacking government troops. The protests originated on the island of Jeju where brutal oppression from the government brought 30,000 deaths, half of them civilians.

A rebellion in October 1948 in the southwest corner of the mainland peninsula vented furious opposition against pro-government families, triggering violent suppression of the pro-communist uprising

ABOVE: Chiang Kai-shek succeeded Sun Yat-sen and fought against the rising popularity of the communist party led by Mao Zedong, but the two joined forces to fight the Japanese invaders. Here, Generalissimo and Madame Chiang Kai-shek share a joke with Lt Gen Joseph W Stilwell commanding the China Expeditionary Forces. (US DoD)

and further bloodshed. Both rebellions had been extinguished by spring 1949 with great loss of life and discontent grew with pro-communist cells maintaining their opposition and government troops battling with several assaults on selective enclaves which calmed the insurgency by early 1950. The violent opposition to South Korea's pro-liberal government, closely aligned as it was with the United States, gave Stalin hope when Kim visited Moscow in March 1949 seeking approval for an all-out invasion, but the Soviet leader urged caution.

The first active measure from the tripartite pact of Russia, China and North Korea was taken by Stalin in May 1950 when he judged the time was right and Moscow gave Kim approval for an all-out invasion. China had reservations, fearing it could be dragged into a war with the Americans, but was heavily dependent on Russia for physical and material resources to power its drive for economic and industrial growth. On the balance of risk, it conceded approval. With agreement secure, Moscow sent its top generals and military advisers to brief Kim and educate the North Korean army leadership in strategy and tactics it had evolved during the war against Nazi Germany.

Across the border, and despite the fact that South Korean military training had been structured by the US Army for a counter-insurgency role rather than as a defensive force against invasion, the US Korean Military Advisory Group were confident that the South Korean army could easily suppress an invasion and Syngman Rhee recklessly toyed with the idea of taking control of North Korea. The CIA believed there was little risk of the North invading the South and discounted reported mass movements to the border as merely a defensive posture on their part. The Americans had made little military preparation for a conflict and considered their role advisory, providing the South Koreans with only small-arms and no heavy armour or mechanised vehicles. It rated low on the trigger alert for the US defensive sphere of interest as worked out between President Truman and his foreign policy advisers.

ABOVE: Chiang Kai-shek (right) and Mao Zedong toasting the end of the war with the Japanese against which they had combined their forces to defeat the invader. However, they would soon resume their military contest for control of China. (Author's collection)

Conversely, shortly after the revolution had brought the communists to power in China, Mao Zedong had begun to send aid and military equipment to North Korea together with army veterans supplementing aircraft, armoured vehicles and tanks sent from Russia. With a population of 9.6 million, North Korea had less than half the population of the South but crucially it had a far better prepared military. In the build up to the invasion Russia had supplied North Korea with 274 tanks, 200 artillery pieces, 132 combat aircraft and more than 135,000 troops in eight infantry divisions and three border constabulary brigades for a potential invasion. However, while the hardware was utilised, the Russian manpower didn't ultimately cross the border and notably the aircraft supplied were vintage types and none of them were jets.

In contrast, the South Koreans could mobilise only 98,000 troops, of which only two-thirds were combat-ready, together with 22 aircraft useful only for liaison and training. The Americans had denied a request for tanks as they gave the probability of war a very low rating. A Top Secret report from Far East Command intelligence believed that "there will be no civil war in Korea this spring or summer", asserting that the most probable action would be "guerrilla activities and psychological warfare." However, other intelligence reports were closer to reality, believing that South Korea was vulnerable, and that the country could fall "whenever Soviet strategy so dictates."

Kremlin officials kept a watching brief on preparations for the invasion, reporting to Stalin that the concentration of North Korean troops had begun on June 12, 1950, and were complete by the 23rd, as laid out by the General Staff. It also verified that the North Korean troops were informed that South Korea had begun an attack and that their response would liberate an oppressed people. The troops were in their attack positions by midnight on June 24.

ABOVE: North Korean leader Kim Il Sung hosted by Soviet army leaders in the immediate aftermath of World War Two, where the Russia took advantage of the defeat of Japan to occupy the country and support an attack on South Korea. (onekorea.ru)

FIRST STRIKE

The attack began at 4:40am on Sunday, June 25, when an artillery barrage opened up and North Korean infantry poured across the border. Forty-five minutes later, two

ABOVE: South Korean leader Syngman Rhee was elected to office in a vote held on May 10, 1948, seen here with General Douglas MacArthur on August 15 inaugurating the newly-formed republic. (Author's collection)

amphibious landings occurred along the east coast south of Kangnung, putting two battalions of marine infantry ashore together with around a thousand partisans. South Korea began firing on the ships, to no avail, and a city further south was captured within hours. Across the border, tanks rolled south with apparent impunity while propeller-driven attack aircraft flew support and strafed the roads and village communities.

The operation had been so meticulously planned that the type of tanks supplied were within the known weight limits of South Korean bridges. Although only lightly armoured they were impervious to the pathetic anti-tank weapons fielded in defence. Russian-inspired tactics laid a carpet of fire from ground attack and by air, with deep strikes carried out by light bombers. Within three hours they were up to three miles (5km) south of the border and by the end of the first day they had advanced a further 7.5 miles (12km). Key to North Korea's military objectives was the capital city Seoul, 35 miles (56km) from the border, possession of which could unseat the South Korean government.

The South Koreans had nothing to equal, or to counter, the North Korean firepower built up by the Russians in the preceding 18 months since the elections signalled a theoretical Russian departure. The Russians had kept their word and gone, their presence replaced with munitions, armour, and all the trappings of a well-equipped fighting force. China had released into North Korea many of the country's former citizens and there were several thousand reserve troops ready to supplement the invasion force.

Because there is a time difference of 14 hours between Korea and the East Coast of the United States the first word of the invasion arrived in the US State Department at 9:26pm on the evening of Saturday, June 24, in a message from Ambassador John J Muccio in Seoul. This was quickly relayed to the Department of Defense and to President Truman who was at Independence, Missouri, as well as to the UN Secretary General Trygve Lie, at his home in Forest Hills, Long Island, New York. Lie informed the State Department that he was prepared to assemble the Security Council to discuss the matter. The following morning, he received a full report from Dr Liu Yu-wan who chaired the liaison committee governing Korean affairs.

The Security Council met on June 25 and passed a unanimous resolution calling for an "immediate cessation of hostilities" and for the North Koreans to withdraw their "armed forces to the 38th parallel." Delivering counsel, the previous evening that the President's presence in Washington DC was probably not needed, Secretary of State Dean Acheson began to change his mind around midday and during dinner, Truman received a telephone call from him to reassess the situation and propose that the President was needed in the capital after all. He landed at 7:15pm that evening and assembled key members of the cabinet and the defence staff at his temporary residence, Blair House.

ABOVE: US President Truman signs the emergency act after North Korea invaded South Korea on June 25, 1950. (NARA)

"While mindful of the death and destruction suffered by the Chinese people between 1937 and 1945, Mao felt no affiliation with the United States which had played a role in defeating the Japanese."

Over dinner, Truman decided that he would not make concerted decisions that evening but would rely on General Douglas MacArthur to get the US Seventh Fleet into action from the Philippines. There was no consensus as to how events might play out or any agreement on the next course of action the United States might take. The following day the news was bleak: the North Koreans had ignored the UN directive and were moving south quickly. A veteran of the two world wars, former superintendent of the West Point military academy and recipient of the Japanese surrender on behalf of the United States, MacArthur was the obvious choice for command of UN forces in Korea.

What was still required was a UN mandate to employ force to expel the North Korean invaders and that finally came on June 27, following which US forces were mobilised for the defence of South Korea. Ill prepared, short of equipment, and with at first a force of only 500 to engage the enemy, over the next several months the US would see a transformation in the way it addressed requirements. In the US, Truman would seize control of the American railroad and steel industries to offset the effects of strikes and a special Act of Congress allowed the government to compel industry to prioritise war materiel. For the first time in five years, America was back spearheading an international force but this time with totally inadequate resources.

CONFRONTATION TO CONTAINMENT

When North Korea attacked its neighbour to the south on June 25, 1950, it invaded a country that until the division at the 38th parallel only five years previously had been shared by a common people. What divided them was two very different ideologies imposed by the victorious powers in 1945. As a result, Syngman Rhee in the South, and Kim Il-sung in the North each wanted to invade the other's country to unite the people and achieve supreme rule over all 29.6 million citizens.

With two-thirds of the country's population but only a fraction of the weapons, soldiers and equipment of the North, South Korea was highly vulnerable, kept depleted in military resources by the United States as it feared provocation by arming it for potential use in an offensive over its neighbour. Because of this, when it came, the ferocity of the attack from the North overwhelmed any semblance of defence and within two days Rhee moved the government out of Seoul. On June 28, a key bridge across the Han River was blown up in an attempt to prevent the communists reaching the capital but 4,000 people were on it when it was destroyed. Several hundred drowned and large numbers of South Koreans were left on the wrong side. Seoul fell later that day.

In a fit of desperation, and in an event concealed for several decades, Rhee slaughtered around 100,000 South Koreans believed to be a part of a pro-communist league and a threat to his government. He had already executed around 20,000 before the invasion began and turned on them in an attempt to purge opposition from a group that included many who had collaborated with the Japanese when they ran the peninsula during World War Two. At Daejeon in the west just below the border, a large city surrounded by mountains, 7,000 men, women and children were executed, and their bodies placed in mass graves, an atrocity cynically blamed on the North Koreans.

By June 30, following an intensive and brutal assault from North Korean forces, South Korea had fewer than 22,000 troops left, a quarter of its original manpower, and UN-mandated forces from outside the country were the only means of saving the South. President Truman would explain later that his own motivation for the use of military force was to prevent the communists from being emboldened to "override nations closer to our own shores," adding that "If the communists were permitted to force their way into the Republic of Korea without opposition from the free world, no small nation would have the courage to resist threat and aggression by stronger communist neighbours." It was the very embodiment of Truman's 'domino theory', that if one country were allowed to fall to communism it would doom other countries to the possibility of a similar fate.

Initial involvement by UN-mandated forces reflected the poorly equipped nature of those initially sent to South Korea, a situation that changed significantly as the North Koreans swept all before them in their charge to the south coastal areas of the region. The quickest way to stem the tide was first to establish air superiority, which was quickly achieved through operations from Japan and by the US Navy, followed by an intensive bombing and ground support plan to assist with the flow of ground forces arriving at ports on the south coast.

The capital Seoul had fallen on June 29 and by September 15, 1950, US forces were being squeezed down into a small pocket in the southeastern corner of the country known as the Pusan perimeter from the name of the coastal town. In an area barely

"In a fit of desperation, and in an event concealed for several decades, Rhee slaughtered around 100,000 South Koreans believed to be a part of a pro-communist league."

ABOVE: A Convair B-36D (49-2658) at RAF Lakenheath, Suffolk, England, on January 16, 1951, attracting large crowds and media attention as the USAF shows its air power during heightened tensions with communist forces in Korea. (Dennis Jenkins)

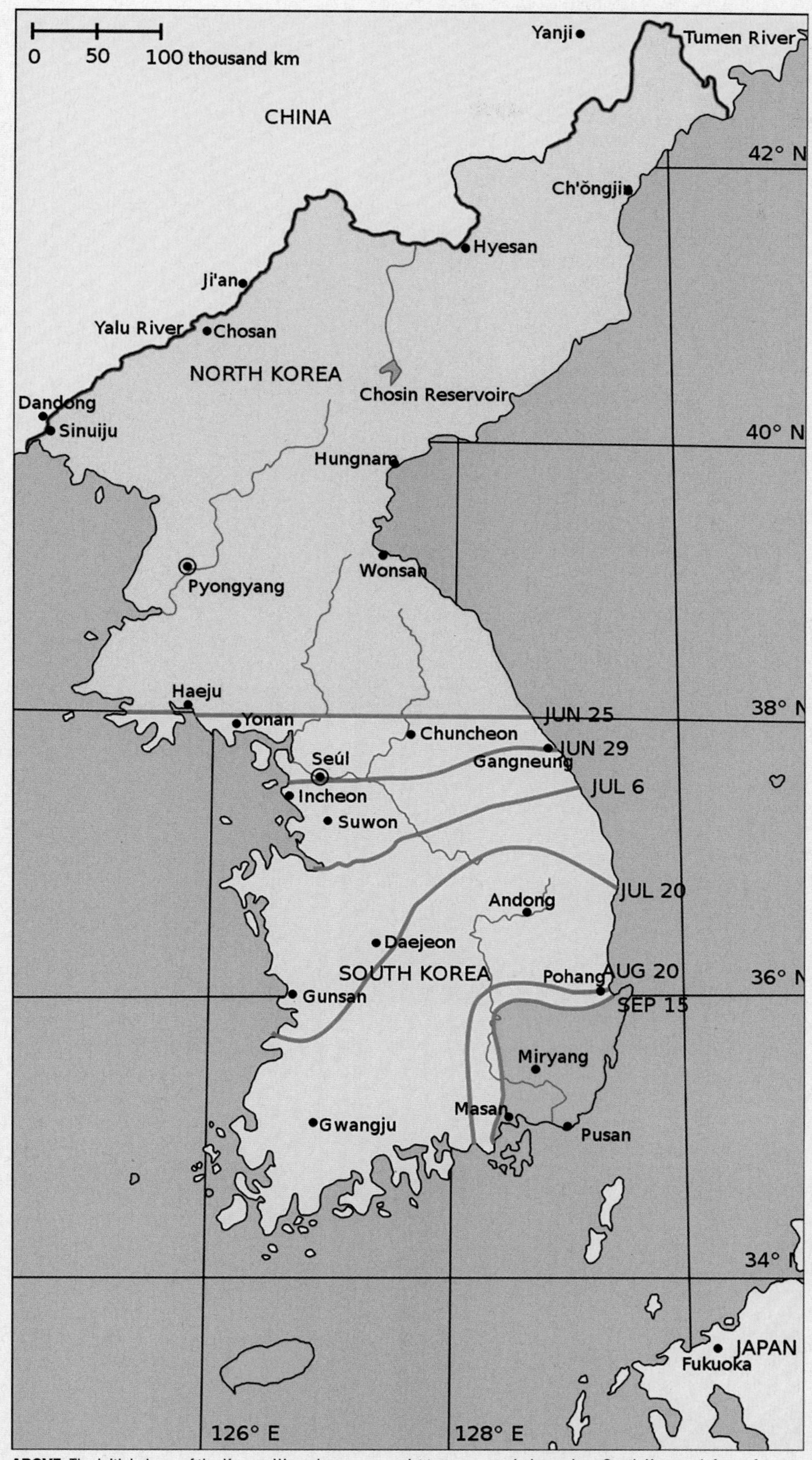

ABOVE: The initial phase of the Korean War, where communist troops overwhelm parlous South Korean defence forces and concentrate resistance around Pusan on the southeast corner of the peninsula. (Author's collection)

70 miles (112km) by 80 miles (129km), the US troops fought back and the breakout from Pusan began on September 16 when the Eighth Army and allies began the long push north. In complete surprise to the communists, a major amphibious landing involving 75,000 troops and 261 ships took place simultaneously on shallow beaches at Inchon, close to the border with North Korea on the western side of the peninsula.

Preceded by massive naval bombardment and intensive air attacks, the operation was a success and Seoul had been liberated by September 25. The push north was a success too, and troops crossed the 38th parallel on October 1. Six days later, MacArthur received word that the UN had approved a total routing of communist forces from South Korea, which he took as tacit approval to invade North Korea. Progress was far greater than anticipated and fearing the worst, on October 1, Kim Il-sung had appealed to Stalin for China's intervention but fearing the consequences the Soviet premier passed it to Mao. On October 19, China entered the war, the day the Americans entered Pyongyang, the capital of North Korea and only 25 miles (40km) north of the 38th parallel.

MacArthur had extended himself beyond the UN mandate and further north than had been authorised by the US government, asserting his plan to push into China to destroy the resources that had supported the North Koreans. The implications of a full-scale war with China were great, as that would likely involve the Soviet Union and a bloody conflict that had no mandate from the United Nations. It would probably bring nuclear weapons into use at a time when Russia had only a handful of atomic bombs and little plausible means of delivering them.

On October 15, 1950, President Truman flew to Wake Island in the Pacific Ocean and met MacArthur for a conference on how to continue the war against North Korea. The US general was left in no doubt that he was not to put boots on Chinese soil and that such a move could start World War Three. However, ignoring the warnings, when Truman returned to the United States, MacArthur sent messages to his commanders urging them to "drive forward with all speed and full utilisation of their force," now introducing UN forces rather than just South Korean units in driving right up to at least the Chinese border. By the end of October, US forces were engaging directly with Chinese army units there.

Intervention by 200,000 Chinese troops across the Yalu River on October 19 had been a unilateral decision and troops from the People's Volunteer Army (PVA), as it was called, moved south during the night, concealing their presence during daylight hours. In 19 days, one division moved south 285 miles (458km). Attacks on UN forces began on October 25 close to the border

"The breakout from Pusan began on September 16 when the Eighth Army and allies began the long push north."

with China, its troops engaging US forces seven days later.

What few people had noticed at the time was a more subtle movement of China's troops into Tibet on October 7, with the goal of annexing the country. While being made to sign agreement to China's rule under duress, and later rescinded because of that, the Dalai Lama appealed for international recognition of his country's independence. It fell on deaf ears and China lodged its explanation with the UN as the 'Peaceful Liberation of Tibet'. Over time, China's military occupation of Tibet would transform the country into a communist state and eliminate an independence movement.

Less veiled was the entry of the Soviet Union into the Korean War. Stalin finally agreed to provide munitions and war materiel to the North Koreans, including their prized jet fighter, the MiG-15. To hide their identity, these aircraft carried North Korean or Chinese air force markings flown by pilots in relevant uniforms or civilian clothes and speaking the associated language off cue-cards in the cockpit. It would be a long time before Russia admitted its participation, but it brought a radical change to the conflict, the first war in which jets flew combat missions against jets. The MiG-15 first appeared on November 1, 1950, when six Soviet jets attacked a flight of F-51 Mustangs.

Most hotly analysed were the sorties in which MiG-15s encountered the flagship of US fighter units, the F-86A Sabre. Most air combat activity with these fighters occurred along the Yalu River close to the border with China. Dubbed 'MiG Alley' by UN pilots, it saw some of the fiercest and most hotly contested engagements of the war. Fearing disclosure of a Russian involvement, Russian pilots were forbidden from flying over UN held territory and under strict instructions not to be taken prisoner if shot down. One downed pilot shot himself to prevent capture and a Russian pilot who ditched in the Yellow Sea was strafed by his own side to prevent him being taken alive.

BELOW: US Army units disembark on the coast of South Korea on August 6, 1950. (US Army)

The aerial feats of both Russian and US pilots have been told many times, but the victory scores reveal the superiority of the F-86 and its pilots. Out of 839 MiG-15s shot down during the war, around 800 were by US pilots in their Sabre jets while the US lost only 58 F-86s to MiG pilots. The US had employed other jet aircraft but 39 of the 40 US air aces credited with five or more victories achieved their 'kills' flying the F-86. However, US pilots were at first surprised to encounter the Russian jet and gave it high marks for performance, manoeuvrability, and the fighting skills of its pilots. Surprise at the technological strides made by Russia drew further concern to that raised when the Soviet Union had detonated its first atomic bomb a year before.

Rapid progress made by Chinese forces ensured their capture of Seoul on January 4, 1951, but UN forces got it back on March 14. During the first six months of 1951, the UN offered China peace negotiations, but they were refused. Pressed by UN forces, Mao appealed to Stalin for additional support and Russia sent two air force divisions and a wide range of equipment. MacArthur suffered a temporary defeat but concerns about

ABOVE: US Army 24th Infantry, one of the exclusively black regiments and originally part of the Buffalo Soldier units, moves up to the front line in South Korea. (US Army)

rocket to launch America's first satellite. Which is perhaps surprising since the Corona programme was well underway and would soon have to be disclosed to the public when flights began. When that did happen in 1959, the rocket was named Discoverer, carrying the cover story that it would conduct research in the biological sciences. However, that did not remain secret for very long and it would soon be disclosed as a spy satellite, albeit with the details remaining highly classified.

But it would be the Russians that launched the Space Age and, from a quick-fire series of spectacular 'firsts' would also launch the Space Race. That happened earlier and faster than anyone had predicted with the Semyorka missile being used to send Sputnik 1 into orbit on October 4, 1957. Responding to this staggering propaganda coup, Vanguard was prepared for a flight attempt which was made on December 6, 1957, but it blew up on the launch pad. Unexpectedly, Sputnik had taken the world by storm and public opinion measured by the US Information Agency around the world showed most countries now believed the Soviet Union would make the greatest progress over the next decade.

Eisenhower gave the army approval to prepare the Redstone for a rapid response and on January 31, 1958, Explorer 1 became the first American satellite to orbit the Earth. Responding with shocked disbelief, Congress held numerous hearings to decide what to do about the Soviet challenge. Two months after launching its first satellite, on December 3, 1957, the Russians had launched Sputnik 2 which carried the dog Laika into orbit and would follow that on May 15, 1958, with Sputnik 3 which had a weight of 2,926lb (1,327kg).

ABOVE: By the mid-1960s the Americans were catching up with Russian space successes and flew 10 missions with the two-man Gemini spacecraft, achieving space-walks, docking in orbit, and flights of up to two weeks in duration. (NASA)

Nobody knew design details of the Semyorka rocket, but the weight this space variant had placed in orbit revealed its enormous size and carrying capacity. With a weight such as this, it could fire a very heavy warhead to the North American continent and that worried a lot of people. It was this that added deep concern to the capabilities of Soviet industry in achieving so much so quickly and that fed back into concerns about their military developments of which nobody in the United States had any realistic knowledge. It was these factors that led Congress to direct the government to set in place policy initiatives that could quickly regain US leadership in these new technologies.

The first US government space policy document was announced in August 1958 with NSC.5814/1 in which the National Aeronautics and Space Administration (NASA) was established and the justification for the civilian space programme was defined. After acknowledging with some alarm that "The USSR has surpassed the United States and the Free World in scientific and technological accomplishments in outer space, which captured the imagination of the world," it succinctly defined the underpinning reason for what would become the Space Race by declaring that it was necessary to "enhance the prestige of the United States among the people of the world and create added confidence in US scientific, technological, industrial and military strength."

Eisenhower saw the space programme both as a civilian endeavour for open and unclassified pursuit of scientific knowledge and as a military capability tuned for gathering detailed intelligence information from spy satellites, for global communication with land forces and for weather forecasting which was crucial for many military operations. Through NASA, the government agency would conduct research as an extension of the science begun with Vanguard, a programme which eventually launched several satellites. But it would be with the use of rockets initially developed for military purposes that NASA and other non-military satellites would be launched.

The US Air Force had an active programme for putting a man in space and when NASA opened its doors for business on October 1, 1958, that programme was handed over to the civilian agency and

BELOW: The recovery of the sixth manned Gemini mission following a rendezvous and docking in space, March 1966. (NASA)

renamed Project Mercury. A tiny capsule capable of carrying a single occupant, it would be test-launched on ballistic flights using a further variant of the Redstone used to launch Explorer 1, and an adapted variant of the Atlas which had greater lifting capacity for placing it in orbit. But those flights would not be ready before 1961 and 1962, respectively, and President Kennedy succeeded Eisenhower in January 1961 with very different ideas.

Meanwhile, as NASA moved ahead with preparations for Mercury and a flotilla of probes for the Moon and the nearer planets, on September 12, 1959, the Russians launched Luna 2 which impacted the Moon. A small sphere weighing 860lb (390kg) carrying the hammer-and-sickle emblem of the USSR on its side, it was intentionally destroyed on impact. This was followed on October 4, 1959, with Luna 3, which looped around the Moon and sent back the first pictures of the far side, also received by the British astronomer Sir Bernard Lovell through the radio tracking station at Jodrell Bank near Manchester, England.

ABOVE: Training for the first Apollo flight, astronauts Virgil Grissom (centre), Ed White (left) and Roger Chaffee died in a fire inside their spacecraft on February 27, 1967. (NASA)

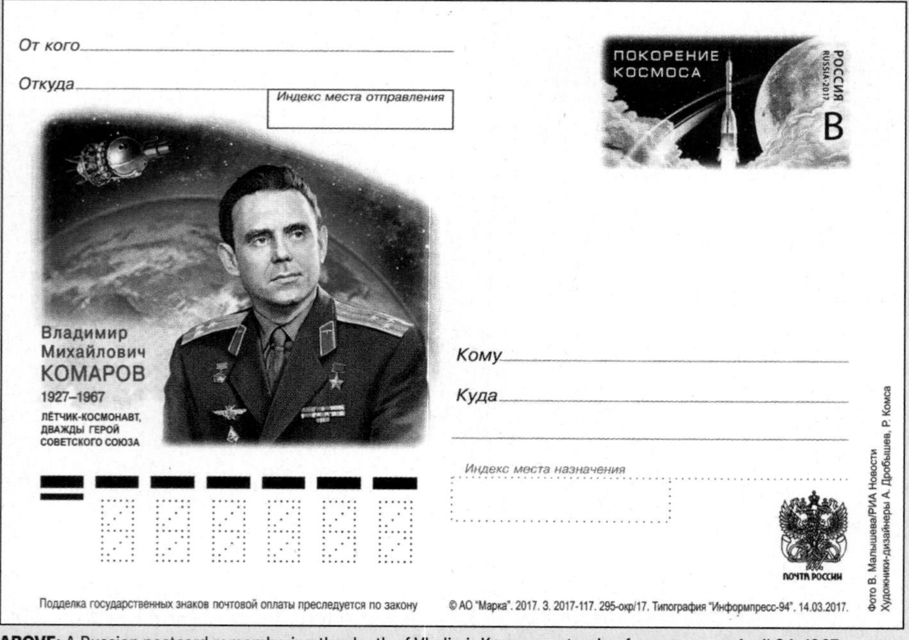

ABOVE: A Russian postcard remembering the death of Vladimir Komarov returning from space on April 24, 1967. (UserGonePostal/Wikimedia)

TO THE MOON!

Kennedy had run for office criticising the Eisenhower administration for lacking the energy to mobilise a stronger response to Soviet achievements in rockets, missile, and space projects, blaming it for a languid pace on existing programmes. In its first year of operation, NASA wanted to plan for a follow-on to Project Mercury and proposed a three-man spacecraft called Apollo which would be capable of conducting science activity in orbit, of sending a crew around the Moon, then into lunar orbit and finally, perhaps landing a man on the Moon by the early 1970s.

Eisenhower did not support this and wanted to see results from Mercury missions before deciding on its successor. At first, Kennedy was of a similar mind although he did increase funding for large Saturn space boosters with performance equal or even exceeding the calculated size and payload lifting capability of equivalent Russian rockets. Eisenhower understood the propaganda value in these projects but was averse to pouring large amounts of money into uncertain goals with unknown value for the nation.

Kennedy was less risk averse and zealous in his determination to put America back on top in science, engineering, and technology, seeing in the space programme one way of using American prowess and the almost inexhaustible capacity of its industrial and research base to put the country ahead of the Soviet Union. But that took a dive on April 12, 1961, when the Russians put Yuri Gagarin in orbit, the first man in space, beating Mercury by some margin. The Kennedy presidency absorbed another humiliating shock five days later when the attempted invasion of Cuba proved an embarrassing failure.

In response to these two defeats, one political and the other propaganda, Kennedy was determined to activate pent national resources and consulted with NASA and other key government agencies about an audacious plan, challenging the Russians to put a man on the Moon by the end of the decade. With congressional approval and with NASA reassuringly confident that it could do that, on May 25, 1961, Kennedy addressed a Joint Session of Congress and the American people asserting that the nation "should commit itself to achieving the goal, before this decade is out, of landing a man on the Moon and returning him safely to the Earth."

Not everyone agreed that this was the right objective for America and more than half of those surveyed in a Gallup poll were opposed to the idea. And the Russians thought so too. Not until 1964, after the death of Kennedy and when faced with a reaffirmation of that commitment across America, did the Soviet Union formally start their own Moon landing programme. But it was too late, and while they struggled to sustain their former record of spectacular

BELOW: Fulfilling President Kennedy's pledge to put astronauts on the Moon by the end of the 1960s, Neil Armstrong and Buzz Aldrin (seen here) achieved that goal on July 20, 1969. (NASA)

successes, the pace of the NASA effort in manned flight exceeded their ability to keep up. After six Mercury missions between 1961 and 1963, 10 manned Gemini flights followed in 1965-66 with docking in space, long duration flights and multiple spacewalks. The last appreciable Soviet space achievement of the 1960s was the world's first spacewalk conducted by Alexei Leonov on a two-man mission in 1965.

But tragedy struck both space-faring nations when three Apollo astronauts died in a fire on the launch pad on January 27, 1967, several weeks prior to flight, and Vladimir Komarov was killed crashing to Earth in his Soyuz capsule on April 24. NASA resumed flights with the first Apollo mission in October 1968 and followed that two months later with the first manned flight into lunar orbit and back. In sending Christmas messages to Earth from around the Moon, the United States asserted a substantial lead in deep-space exploration and followed that three missions later with the first manned landing on the Moon, July 20, 1969.

The Russians turned to development of space stations in which it achieved outstanding successes but the race to the Moon had been won and a new era of coexistence had already been set by both space-faring superpowers. Competition was replaced with cooperation and in July 1975, Russian cosmonauts and American astronauts linked up in orbit to shake hands and ratify a new period in space achievements. After Apollo, Russia continued to expand its space operations with Salyut and Mir stations in Earth orbit and NASA developed the Space Shuttle, with which it planned to build a permanent scientific research facility in orbit.

The Shuttle first flew on April 12, 1981, the 20th anniversary of the flight of Yuri Gagarin. The Russians developed their own shuttlecraft called Buran, but it flew only once on November 15, 1988, before the terminal decline of the Soviet Union and the end of the Cold War brought it down as an unaffordable luxury. By the end of the Cold War the Russians had compiled an unprecedented amount of detailed information about how humans can operate over long periods in space, far exceeding the duration of any NASA flight at the time.

After the collapse of the Soviet Union, the United States and its partners Japan, the European Space Agency and Canada invited the Russians to pool their extensive knowledge and join them in what became the International Space Station (ISS). Assembled partly by Russian rockets and station modules and supplied for many years by Soyuz spacecraft ferrying crewmembers back and forth, the ISS has been permanently manned since 2000 and is destined to remain so for another 10 years. The turbulent and frequently fractious competition that began as a race for the allegiance of politically uncommitted countries evolved into one of the biggest engineering projects of all time, achieved only through the cooperation of people from very different cultures across the globe.

SUPERSONIC WINGS

Britain had been a highly successful exponent of innovative science and engineering concepts immediately before

BELOW: Now on display at Pier 86 in New York, Concorde G-BOAD made its first flight on August 25, 1976, and its last flight took place on November 10, 2003, when it was delivered to the United States. (Aero Icarus/Wikimedia)

"Some of those reports were quite shocking, a very large number of people in a December 1957 report believing that the Soviet Union was the superpower of the future."

ABOVE: Concorde G-BOAB relocated to London-Heathrow at the end of its fleet life. (Simon Boddy)

and during World War Two. Its use of radar in the world's first early-warning system tied to a fully operational air defence network was unique. It involved transmitter-towers of the Chain Home system connecting detection to alert and interception capabilities at fighter stations. Pioneering too was the development by Frank Whittle in Britain of the gas turbine reaction engine, which was simultaneously developed in Germany, but which underpinned the first generation of jet fighters in Britain and the United States while providing Russia with engines to equip its early MiG jet interceptors.

Key in several respects to the development of the atomic bomb had been British scientists and engineers contributing to the US Manhattan Project, which produced the fissile devices tested in Alamogordo, New Mexico and dropped twice on Japanese cities. In immediate post-war Britain the development of an independent nuclear deterrent was pursued as a priority for the Attlee government and further exploited to provide RAF Bomber Command with a lethal inventory of more than 200 nuclear and thermonuclear bombs during the 1960s.

By the end of World War Two, Britain's aeronautical industry was second to none in design and technology applications, albeit only a fraction of the size of that in the United States. Nevertheless, in the mid-1950s studies began in Britain of a supersonic transport (SST) which at first produced scepticism and then positive support as initial design and technology challenges were evaluated and overcome. In seeking to exploit equally innovative thinking, French aeronautical designers developed their own concept for an SST and in 1960 had meetings with their British counterparts with unanimous agreement on the optimal configuration and the requirements for its powerful turbojet engines.

On November 29, 1962, the British and French governments signed an agreement to build what would be called Concorde, a supersonic airliner capable of carrying around 100 passengers at speeds just over Mach 2 – twice the speed of sound. As development progressed the cost escalated and came close to cancellation by the UK Labour government in 1964 despite orders for 74 aircraft from 16 airlines. Taking a non-too subtle approach to eliminate competition, there had been pressure from the American government for Britain to 'look again' at prestige projects such as Concorde when it signed a $3bn financial aid package to Britain on November 25, 1964. While the US saw supersonic airliners as prestige projects, the British saw them as a prudent commercial bid for sales in an exclusive market niche which, when first set up had seemed a wise decision.

Nevertheless, ostensibly on cost grounds, the British government tried to cancel Concorde but the tight contractual deal with France would have incurred a higher withdrawal fee than the cost of completion. The only voice in the cabinet supporting Concorde was Tony Benn, a member of the Labour government under Harold Wilson. There had been several reasons for concern in the United States, not least because at the time, industrial, economic, and aeronautical opinion believed that SSTs were the airliners of the future.

Fearing the head start by the Anglo-French Concorde project, President Kennedy pushed hard for US industry to produce a competitive SST to challenge what his government perceived to be an impending monopoly lost to the British. Of equal concern was the ascendency of a European aerospace industry capable of challenging the United States in trade and manufacturing, further influencing support from the developing world which the United States sought to attract and whose cooperation it sought to retain a trading monopoly in goods and natural resources.

Three days after the Concorde deal was signed by Britain and France in 1962, the boss of the US Federal Aviation Agency (now Administration), Najeeb Halaby urged Kennedy to immediately begin an SST project, citing predicted job losses of 50,000 from the aviation industry and $7bn in revenue and capital if it did nothing. Moving fast, seeking a pre-eminent position to maintain its dominant position in the commercial aviation market, requests for bids from three airframe builders in 1964 estimated a market for 500 SSTs by 1990. Boeing got the contract, and a series of design proposals changed the configuration of the aircraft over time.

Watching closely and intent on surpassing Western achievements, the Soviet Union funded studies into its own SST and began formal development of what would

ABOVE: Seen here at the 1975 Paris Air Show, Tupolev developed the Tu-144 during the 1960s in parallel with the Anglo-French Concorde supersonic transport. (Michael Gilland)

become the Tupolev Tu-144 on July 26, 1963. Dubbed 'Koncordski' after its overall visual similarity to Concorde, it was to be capable of carrying 150 passengers at Mach 2.15, a little faster than its Anglo-French competitor. With high political pressure to get in the air ahead of Concorde, the development was rushed, and corners were cut but it achieved its first flight on December 31, 1968, ahead of Concorde which got airborne on March 2, 1969.

With considerable development still ahead of it, the Tu-144 went into service on December 26, 1975, but only for freight and mail from Moscow to Alma-Ater, a distance of 1,950 miles (3,137km) and it began passenger operations on November 1, 1977. Concorde flights had already begun, the first being London-Bahrain and Paris-Rio de Janeiro via Dakar on January 21, 1976. Neither aircraft was successful and only the national carriers, Aeroflot in Russia, British Airways in the UK, and Air France operating an SST. No other country has developed and operated a supersonic transport system. Aeroflot halted services in 1978 after 102 'commercial' flights. One Tu-144 crashed at the Paris Air Show on June 3, 1973, with the loss of all 14 on board and an Air France Concorde crashed at Paris Charles de Gaulle airport on July 25, 2000, killing all 109 passengers and crew and four people on the ground. Air France last flew Concorde on June 27, 2003, when one was delivered to retirement at Toulouse and British Airways retired theirs on October 24.

What had begun as a commercial investment in 1962 for the UK and France prompted a new chapter in the race for technological supremacy by the United States and the Soviet Union, neither prepared to concede to the other a prestige project that channelled national assets into a flagship propaganda project. At least Russia's Tu-144 entered service, albeit briefly. The US SST never materialised and deemed uneconomic, the project was cancelled in 1971. By that time, environmental awareness was growing fast in America and the polluting effects of stratospheric flight, and the disrupting effect of the overland sound barrier brought nationwide lobbies for it to be dropped.

ABOVE: In flight with the nose drooping, the Tu-144 was never a truly commercial success but was employed as an example of Soviet technical capabilities. (Novosti)

The more empowering reason why it failed was also why Concorde was never a commercial success, only 14 ever operated by its national carriers. While developing its SST, Boeing was also building the world's biggest airliner, the Boeing 747 – popularly known as the jumbo jet. With capacity for more than 400 people in its developed evolution, the jumbo offered low seat prices and opened new opportunities for people previously outpriced from flying to holiday destinations.

Simultaneously, an oil crisis, wars in the Middle East and high interest rates turned users and operators away from fuel-hungry modes of transportation. The number of miles flown per passenger on one unit of fuel was five times higher for the Jumbo Jet than for Concorde. SSTs were simply too expensive to buy, far too expensive to operate and there were too few people willing to pay $12,000 to cross the Atlantic.

For nine years a flight attendant on Concorde, Joe Cuddy remembers the experience: "The atmosphere in the cabin was one of an exclusive club, and it was because these were the people who controlled the world, controlled the world's finance and the world's trade. It was such an incredibly unique experience, and you were going faster than rifle bullets, twice the speed of sound. It was just a fabulous time."

"Post-war, rocketry and the possibility of space travel became a serious study and put both Russia and America into an arms race with military, political and propaganda value."

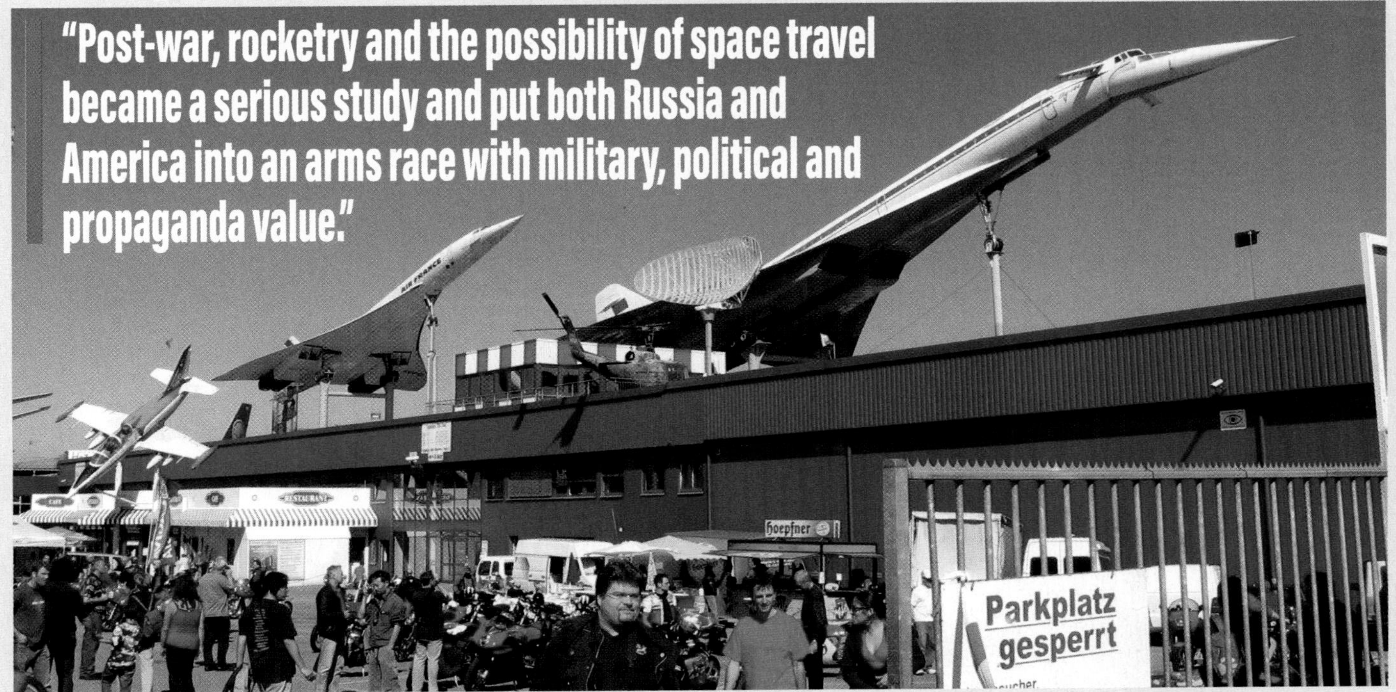

ABOVE: Displayed at the Sinsheim Auto & Technik Museum in Germany, full scale replicas of the Air France Concorde (left) and the Aeroflot Tu-144 make a spectacular rooftop adornment! (Marcin Wichary)

FROM CONTAINMENT TO COEXISTENCE

The Cold War posed serious challenges to the United States and its allies and to the Soviet Union and ideologically aligned countries around the world. For five years after the end of World War Two, both countries built their respective societies around vastly different societal principles, while each saw the other as antagonistic and expansionist. Two seminal events hardened the line against communism – the rise to power of the Marxist-Leninist Mao Zedong in China and the Korean War of 1950-53 which entered a period of suspended confrontation through the armistice.

Inheriting the US presidency from Roosevelt's death on April 12, 1945, Harry Truman presided over early post-war readjustments and suffered as a result of facing some of the toughest decisions of office: how to transform a nation from four years of war to a lasting peace, redefining the foreign policy of the nation and seeing the country through a major transformation in the way the economy received and spent its income. His popularity fell from 82% when he was sworn in to 36% when he stood for re-election in 1948, yet Truman made one of the most outstanding come-backs in US presidential history by beating Republican candidate Thomas Dewey and taking 28 of the 48 states.

ABOVE: The US National Security Council is a high office within the Executive Office of the President, and it was NSC-68 that defined the strategic and geopolitical policy of the United States throughout the Cold War. (The White House)

ABOVE: Paul Nitze (left) graduated from Harvard University in 1928 and after a period as investment banker he served under President Truman in the Department of States advocating regime change in rogue states and 'rollback', a process of intervention. (US State Department)

He immediately faced more crises. The Berlin airlift was in the deep chill of winter and getting supplies to the beleaguered citizens of Germany's former capital was a huge political and logistical undertaking. Also, in October 1949 Mao proclaimed the People's Republic of China. Aid to Chiang Kai-shek's nationalists, including US Marines fighting to keep the communists down, had been stopped in December 1948 in the belief that a full military intervention would be required to prevent the communists taking over the country, an area supporting a quarter of the world's population. Chiang fled to Formosa, now known as Taiwan, and any opportunity for a full-scale intervention had gone.

Truman had already supported a tough line on Soviet Russia and its demands, outlining that as the Truman Doctrine on March 12, 1947, reiterated with greater emphasis on July 4, 1948, telling Congress that it must "be the policy of the United States to support free peoples who are resisting attempted subjugation by armed minorities or by outside pressures."

and 58,220 Americans were killed between 1965 and 1976.

In neighbouring Cambodia, the Khmer Rouge overran the country and seized power in 1975, changing its name to Kampuchea and bringing a brutal and repressive regime, abolishing schools, temples, hospitals, and libraries in pursuit of Maoist doctrine and farm systems based on practices from the 11th century. Large swathes of the population were punished and up to two million murdered for their racial, ethnic, or social position in a regime which persecuted those with an education or 'Western' ideas. The country was closed completely to the outside world, the infamous 'killing fields' being places used for mass executions, which included medical, legal, and pseudo-industrial professionals in a total war on intellectualism.

After three years of border harassment, in November 1978 the Khmer Rouge was defeated when Vietnamese armed forces invaded, and a pro-Soviet state established as the Kampuchean People's Revolutionary Party. The monarchy was restored in 1993, Sihanouk returned to the throne and the country entered a time of relatively peaceful democratic conditions, notwithstanding the occasional uprising and coup that failed to return the country to the oppressions and brutality of its years under the Khmer Rouge. In December 1975, the monarchy in neighbouring Laos was overthrown and the country was renamed the Lao People's Democratic Republic expressing special cooperation with Vietnam, which remains under the communist regime.

ABOVE: In a desperate bid to force North Vietnam to sue for peace, President Nixon goes on TV to explain why he is expanding the war into Cambodia. (The White House)

While US intervention in southeast Asia from 1965 produced conflict across three countries lasting 20 years, the British held fast for 12 years to their own former colony, Malaysia. Situated between Thailand, its land border to the north with Indonesia to its south and west, the Malay Peninsular was a Portuguese colony from 1511, under the Dutch from 1641 and the British from 1786, all three laying claim to different parts of the country. After the wartime occupation by the Japanese between 1942 and 1945, the British plan to administrate the country under the Malayan Union attracted opposition from the population and it was replaced by the Federation of Malaya in February 1948, essentially still under British rule.

Operating internally, a large number of the Chinese Malay formed guerrilla groups under the national communist party with help from Beijing and a long and protracted campaign against them was organised by the British in what became known as the Malayan Emergency. The communist National Liberation Army organised a military campaign against the British in what was a similar uprising to that which the Americans had faced prior to 1965. The British Army and the RAF was involved in a fierce and protracted struggle to control villages but on September 8, 1955, the Federation declared an amnesty for communist activists.

Despite a campaign to encourage support for the government, the communists failed to take advantage of this and melted away, many fleeing across the border to Thailand. Their bid failed because the British were ever willing to settle the struggle through engagement and compromise. On August 31, 1957, Malaya became an independent member of the Commonwealth and on July 31, 1960, the British declared the 'emergency' over, ending a period during which 1,443 British and 1,346 Malayan troops had been killed together with 6,710 guerrillas and almost 2,500 civilians.

In what could be regarded as a struggle for independence, the Malayan Emergency can also be considered as a proxy war in that it sought to stem communist factions from taking over control of the country and was therefore one additional domino in the game of geopolitical politics which saw much of the Free World supporting those policy objectives. The 30 years of conflict that brought war to southeast Asia was a consequence of unsettled struggles between communism, fascism, Nazism, and a struggle for colonialism that had begun before World War Two. Unsettled, those struggles had brought violent uprisings for more than three decades after the Japanese had been driven out.

ABOVE: A US Navy LTV-7E Corsair II from the USS *Kitty Hawk* delivers a strike on the bridge over the Hai Duong River during Operation Linebacker. (USN)

SPOOKS AND TUNNELS

The Cold War was energised through perceived threats. By the Americans and most of the Western World on the possibility that the Soviet Union was seeding communism around the world and might just resort to conflict to achieve its aims. The Soviet Union believed that most of the West and the politically uncommitted world was plotting its downfall. Both viewpoints were true but not in the way, or for the reasons, that fuelled fear – fear being the mobilising force throughout the period of international tension from 1945 to 1990. At the core was the need to know what was going on in countries opposed to national objectives and policies of either side and sometimes even inside the nation states of the two opposing ideologies. All the major players in the Cold War had sophisticated intelligence-gathering organisations.

The British had MI5, formed on October 7, 1909, as the national counter-intelligence and security organisation set up primarily to monitor German threats and to ensure the protection of British citizens. It was partnered with the existing MI6, operational from July 4, 1909, as the Secret Service Bureau and later as the Secret Intelligence Service (SIS) for obtaining information about foreign powers. A key legacy of World War Two, the Government Communications Headquarters (GCHQ) based at Cheltenham, England, is a direct outgrowth of the code-breaking Bletchley Park and does a similar job with signals intelligence (SIGINT).

Predominant in operating throughout the Cold War, in the United States the Central Intelligence Agency was established by President Truman on September 18, 1947, with responsibilities similar to those of MI6. It owes its origin to elements of British intelligence with whose help it was set up. Following this on November 4, 1952, the National Security Agency (NSA) has responsibility for global intelligence gathering, collation and analysis. Specialising in integrating human intelligence (HUMINT) and SIGINT, the NSA provides guidance rather than acquisition other than that which derives from its own programmes, usually expedited by other agencies.

President Kennedy authorised two new organisations in 1961, the Defence Intelligence Agency (DIA) to serve combat requirements and the National Reconnaissance Office (NRO) to manage spy satellites, an organisation kept secret for many years. The DIA conducts covert and clandestine intelligence gathering for the use of the Department of Defense and reports directly to the secretary of defense and, since 2004, to the director of national intelligence. This is a cabinet-level position to whom all the US intelligence agencies report for integrating the separate strands of information and presenting a unified picture to the political leadership.

Intelligence-gathering is of either an overt or a covert type: overt intelligence harvests useful information from open and readily available material. Sources include official statements, conversations with a country's powerbase, printed or electronic media and through the open exchange of unclassified material across borders; covert intelligence gathers classified or restricted information obtained by clandestine means from a foreign country or its representatives and that can involve the use of unlawful activity in a foreign country.

Hybrid intelligence-gathering combines overt and covert sources to inform

> "The Central Intelligence Agency was established by President Truman on January 22, 1946, with responsibilities similar to those of MI6."

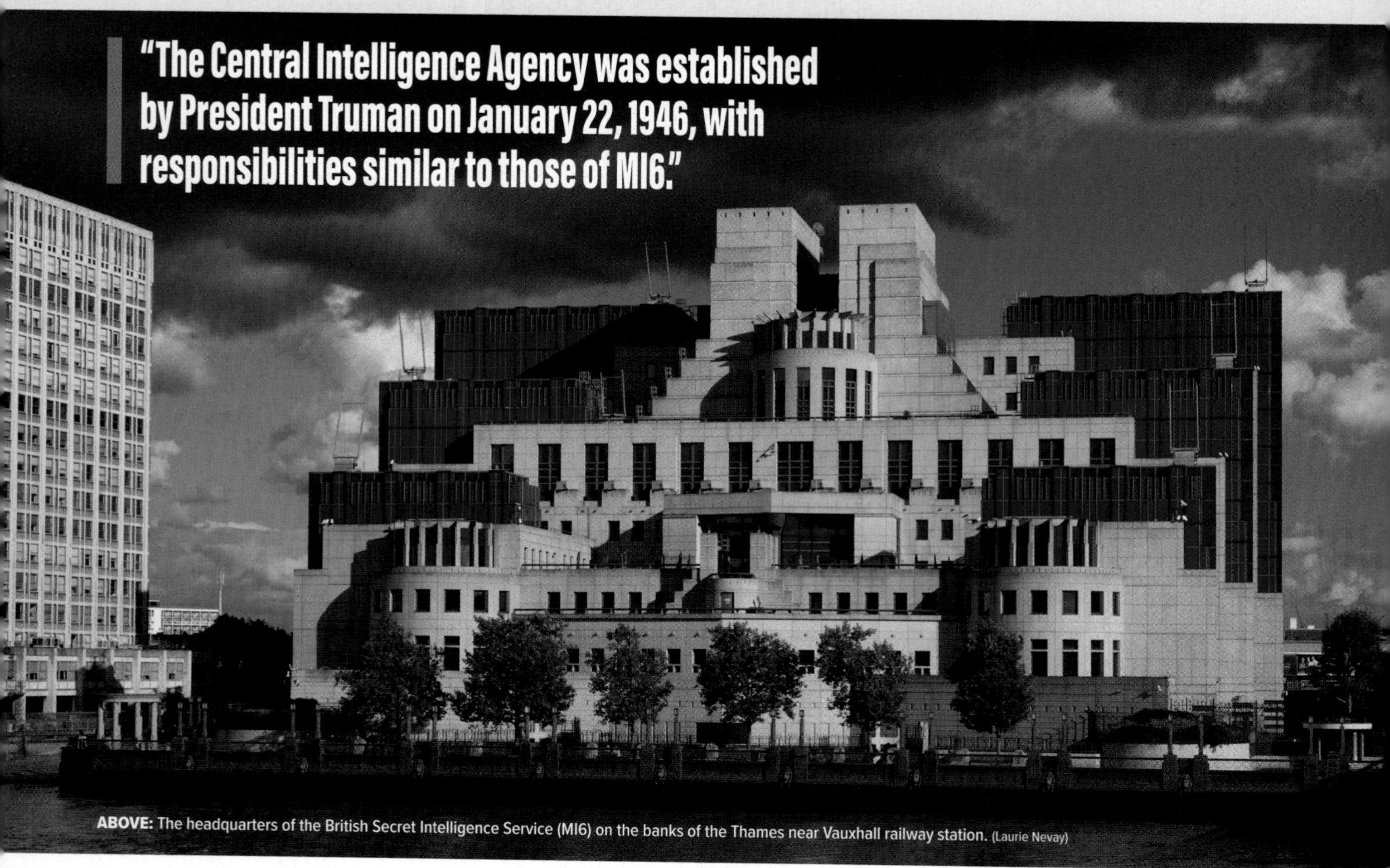

ABOVE: The headquarters of the British Secret Intelligence Service (MI6) on the banks of the Thames near Vauxhall railway station. (Laurie Nevay)

ABOVE: The cyber-security centre in England is the GCHQ headquarters outside Cheltenham, which handles signals-intelligence information from around the world and is connected to receiving stations in the UK and in other places. (GCHQ)

appropriate national agencies about threats to its citizens and to assess the possibility and sometimes, if accurate or just plain lucky, the probability of attacks on a country or its people. The use of overt and covert intelligence gathering had an 'open' purpose too and during the Cold War was valuable for assessing trends and political orientation of large populations of interest to diplomats and embassies in foreign countries. It provided the CIA with manufacturing, production, agricultural output, and a range of information about the true state of a country and its economy.

As noted in a previous chapter, the establishment of the United States Information Agency (USIA) in 1953 provided an opportunity to gather open information from around the world, to garner details of how people were living their lives and what they were thinking, what they were doing and what they were spending their money on. In the Cold War, polls funded by the USIA innocuously trawled the average citizen in a way that would make today's social media data-harvesting a very energy intensive way of getting useful information.

Throughout the Cold War, information obtained from open sources was used to mobilise propaganda campaigns for government messages, either to its own people or to citizens in other countries. All major countries transmitted foreign language broadcasts on frequencies reaching targeted audiences for propaganda purposes. The largest of these being the Voice of America (VOA) from the United States, Radio Moscow from the Soviet Union, and the BBC World Service from the UK. So pervasive were these broadcasts that some countries tried to jam transmissions or made it illegal to listen in, and that still exists in some totalitarian states.

Propaganda is categorised by three separate definitions: 'white' propaganda which is officially sanctioned spin on government policy, a bending of rules and facts and the use of statistical nuance to shape public perception of a policy or a viewpoint to positive advantage; 'black' propaganda is covert and subversive bending of truth or setting out lies to attack an opponent or an opposing view so as to erode credibility; 'grey' propaganda lies somewhere in between the two and is arguably the most dangerous. This is because challengers to a given message can be deflected by selecting true facts to divert attention away from asserted facts that are actually lies. In this way, 'facts' mixed in with 'untruths' can be presented so as to appear that the entire gamut of the declared view or policy is genuine, without having to assess it against a menu of both kinds, which can then erode confidence.

THE PRACTITIONERS

Schooled in evasion and obfuscation by his experiences in World War Two, Eisenhower was arguably the first modern leader to use propaganda to influence the way the general public viewed national policies and the decisions made by government.

> "Throughout the Cold War, information obtained from open sources was used to mobilise propaganda campaigns for government messages."

He applied to American voters, techniques which had previously been used by former Presidents exclusively to shape the way foreign countries saw the United States. It was a functional part of his administration, embracing the way the world saw America and the way the electorate saw its leadership.

In explaining this, Eisenhower wrote: "A great deal of this particular type of thing would be done through arrangements with all sorts of privately operated enterprises in the field of entertainment, dramatics, music, and so on and so on. Another part of it would be done through clandestine arrangements with magazines, newspapers and other periodicals, and book publishers, in some countries. The entire part must be carefully segregated, in my opinion, from the official statement of (the) American position before the world."

On the question of how this should be articulated, he said that there must be no "real or apparent connection" between the various forms of propaganda and in April 1959 he directed the USIA boss George Allen that all these forms should be "infiltrated into local radio stations and performed by people other than Americans" so as to enhance plausibility but that to "insert such propaganda of course, such matters as bribery, etc, would have to be indulged in."

Initially, these techniques were developed for obtaining intelligence about activities

ABOVE: An MI6 informant who provided much vital information about Soviet missile developments and other national security information, Oleg Gordievsky converses with President Ronald Reagan on July 21, 1987. (Mary Anne Fackelman/Ronald Reagan Presidential Library)

BELOW: The National Security Agency (NSA) in the United States was established in 1952 and is the world's largest crypto-analytical organisation. This view of its headquarters at Fort Meade, Maryland, was taken in 1985 before considerable expansion of its facilities and capabilities. (NSA)

in foreign countries, especially those under communist rule and perceived to be a threat to the United States and its allies. Government agents operating as spies came through different channels. US embassies had staff with named positions hiding their true function as spies, going around their assigned countries on diplomatic business, obtaining information from overt activities. The Russians had exactly the same pseudo-diplomats operating in the West. Others, on both sides, were operating in these countries in covert ways, people often recruited from civilian professions spying on activities and reporting back what they saw and what they were able to find out.

At a deeper level to these 'legals' were 'illegals', individual Russian people and sometimes families living and working in Western countries but gathering information in their daily lives. Some illegals had migrated to America in the late 1930s as a result of proclaimed persecution under Stalin and some had been sent over with tall tales to give them a welcome in their new home. There were instances of sons and daughters of immigrants working in classified positions due to their longevity of residence, there to spy and send information to Moscow. There was also an intricate network of double-agents in Moscow who continued to provide information to operatives passing information back to the West via other intermediaries.

When Oleg Gordievsky, former head of KGB operations in London defected in July 1985 after serving as a double-agent for 12 years, he told the British authorities about a massive spy network operating in the UK. He managed to get away only hours before he would have been arrested and got to England in safety, escaping execution. But he left behind his family and contacted Prime Minister Margaret Thatcher seeking help to pressure the Russians into letting them leave. Receiving reassurance, great pressure was brought on Moscow at a time when relations were warming through the liberal policies of Mikhail Gorbachev, but the KGB refused to let them go.

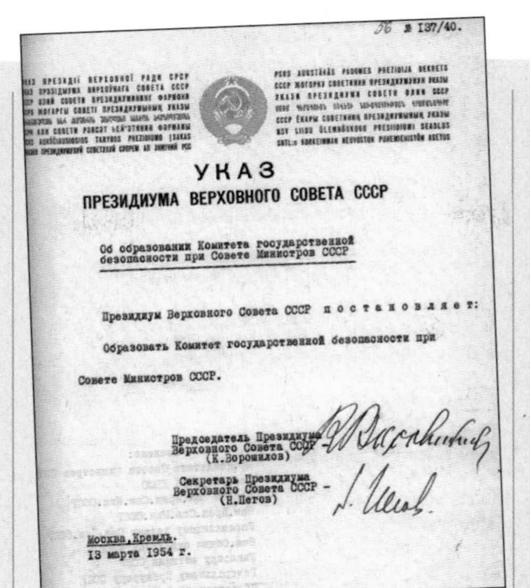

№ 137/40.

УКАЗ

ПРЕЗИДИУМА ВЕРХОВНОГО СОВЕТА СССР

Об образовании Комитета государственной безопасности при Совете Министров СССР

Президиум Верховного Совета СССР постановляет:

Образовать Комитет государственной безопасности при Совете Министров СССР.

Председатель Президиума Верховного Совета СССР - (К.Ворошилов)

Секретарь Президиума Верховного Совета СССР - (Н.Пегов)

Москва, Кремль.
13 марта 1954 г.

ABOVE: The document that brought the KGB into existence in 1954, supplanting the former NKVD which masterminded terror campaigns across the Soviet Union. (K E Voroshilov)

That September, incensed at the rebuff and having sent Gordievsky messages of hope, Margaret Thatcher ordered 25 Russian diplomats to leave the UK. These were legals, some of whom were also integrating communication networks with illegals. It brought a reciprocal response and the British embassy in Moscow lost 25 of its own staff. When a further six Russians were ordered to leave London, six British diplomats were ordered out of the Soviet Union. Stripping out almost all the staff at the British embassy, Ambassador Sir Bryan Cartledge was not impressed: "Never engage in a pissing match with a skunk, he possesses important natural advantages."

Forcible thinning out in the British Embassy was painful. The departed consisted of legitimate diplomatic staff, British journalists including the BBC's Tim Sebastian and two MI6 officers who had smuggled Gordievsky out of Moscow to Finland in the boot of a car. In selecting those ordered to leave the country, the Soviets picked staff who could speak Russian, thus incurring extended damage until they could be replaced through lengthy applications.

All the while, a range of contacts in Russia who were sympathetic to the West continued to receive visits and gifts from business people working through trade organisations set up by the CIA or MI6 as a cover. In several cases these Russians never conducted espionage activities or carried out spying activity but were simply part of a lost group known as the 'forever people' whose grandparents had fought to save Russia from the communists after World War One.

One of those whose parents had been killed fighting German soldiers in World War Two still kept mementoes her family had received from Tsar Nicholas II before he was murdered in July 1918. She waited, quietly for the day when communism would collapse, and she could walk the streets wearing her brooches and earrings. One day, in the Gorbachev period, she did just that. But it was too soon, and those adornments were recognised, and she was attacked in the street.

During the Cold War Russia developed the world's largest spy network of modern times and placed several hundred legals and illegals around the globe. Internally, the Soviet Union established a system for spying on its own people to find subversive elements and to remove people working against the system, even those merely expressing opposing views. In several East European countries, police forces had their own ways of finding disruptive elements. Most famous was the Stasi, active in East Germany, the German Democratic Republic (GDR). Mirrored on the KGB, it was highly effective, brutal in its activities and active in extreme torture

The Stasi, technically the GDR's secret intelligence service had been set up immediately after the war employing former Nazis schooled in Soviet practices by the KGB. Notionally independent from Moscow from 1957 it continued to operate with offices in Leningrad and Moscow to keep a close eye on East German tourists. A notable

BELOW: The KGB and its military equivalent the GRU supported national security services set up in East European countries loyal to the Soviet Union. The Stasi had its notorious headquarters in Berlin where many people suffered at the hands of interrogators. (Stasi Museum)

ABOVE: From the earliest days of the Cold War, the United States had a warfighting plan should it need to attack the Soviet Union, this map showing targets in Russia and Manchuria identified as key to eliminating the ability of Russia to sustain a conflict. (USAF)

end of the Cold War, Trident II has a range of around 7,400 miles (12,000km).

From the beginning of the arms race post-1950, the position in Russia was very different to that in the United States. The general impression in the West gave the Soviet Union credit for greater numbers of offensive weapons than was actually the case. In the mid-1950s there had been the 'bomber-gap' myth in which it was believed that Russia had a superiority in long-range bombers, in their production rates and their potential for attacking the United States. It was an impression specifically tailored by the Russians to deceive the West – and it worked, but only for a while. Then there was the 'missile-gap' myth in which the Russians were believed to have a similar advantage in long-range rockets threatening the West, but that too evaporated with better intelligence.

Nevertheless, the fear in the West of expanding Soviet military capabilities rested largely on the size of the Red Army, most of which was deployed west of the Ural Mountains, and the public perception from their achievements in the Space Race. With the US surging toward a Moon landing, by the mid-1960s that perception had dimmed, and American achievements began to outstrip those of the Soviet Union. In the Soviet military, there was increasing concern that Khrushchev had placed too much reliance on rockets, missiles and 'push-button' warfare, at the cost of conventional forces on land, at sea, and in the air.

After the 1962 Cuban missile crisis, Admiral Gorshkov got the funds he required for a warm-water navy and began a programme of modernisation and shipbuilding to provide a wide-ranging nuclear capability. Alarmed at the build-up of America's Polaris-carrying, nuclear-powered submarine force and its global reach with carrier battle groups, by the mid-1970s Gorshkov had built a completely different navy which could challenge American presence at sea around the world. Gorshkov also presided over the construction of four Kiev-class aircraft carriers equipped with fighter jets and helicopters and in service from 1975. Toward the end of the 1980s, work began on a larger carrier, the *Admiral Kuznetsov* which remained unfinished at the collapse of the Soviet Union. But it had not been in the navy alone that deficiencies had crept in.

> **"For the first five years of the Cold War, tensions smouldered but events failed to persuade a cost-cutting US government to boost defence spending."**

ABOVE: With headquarters at Offutt Air Force Base in Nebraska, and manned penetrating bombers and a force of ICBMs in underground silos, Strategic Air Command held two legs of the nuclear triad throughout the Cold War, the US Navy holding the third with its nuclear-tipped ballistic missiles in submarines. (USAF)

BELOW: Three generations of US bomber. The wartime B-17 (top) was succeeded for raids on Japan by the more advanced B-29 (left), succeeded from the early 1950s by the B-52. (USAF)

Gradually, during the 1960s, the lack of pace both in Soviet air and missile delivery systems became apparent. The parlous state of Russia's ballistic missile programme had not always been known to Western intelligence officials but for a long time it had been suspected. Publicly, that conclusion had been denied so as to support different causes for various political and military reasons. The US Air Force had wanted to paint the grimmest picture of inventories to support claims for higher missile stocks without ever having defined the number of warheads necessary for deterrence. But an earlier study had been known to Washington's military advisers for some time.

In the early days of planning for Britain's nuclear deterrent an extensive assessment determined that a stockpile of 200 atomic bombs was sufficiently credible to deter a Soviet attack and that had defined the size of the RAF's V-bomber force. When in 1963 the UK accepted the American Polaris missile for British-built, nuclear- powered submarines, that figure was retained and still forms the backdrop to decisions about the UK's deterrent. But the influence of force deployment levels on American policy during the Kennedy administration completely reshaped national defence planning and international affairs.

ABOVE: As viewed in polar projection, attacks between North America and Russia across the North Pole take the shortest route to strike an opposing country. The need for defence across the Arctic was self-evident, also the path for missiles taking the quickest flight. (Author's collection)

RESHAPED POLICY

When Kennedy came to office in 1961, the alleged missile-gap was only one issue to address. The other was the start of a transformation in the way the strategic defence policies of the United States were configured, in the equipment which would be necessary, and in the way nuclear weapons were regarded. It was nothing less than the birth of an entirely new strategy introducing a radically different concept for deterrence and warfighting.

The Eisenhower administration had set in motion a progressively expanding plan for an increasing number of nuclear weapons, of different types and yields together with a wider range of ships, rockets, and missiles, together with land and air forces that could attack the Soviet Union and communist China.

Land-based missiles in silos included the remaining few Atlas ICBMs as well as Titan II and Minuteman. The US Navy had the Polaris missile deployed in nuclear-powered submarines and the US Air Force

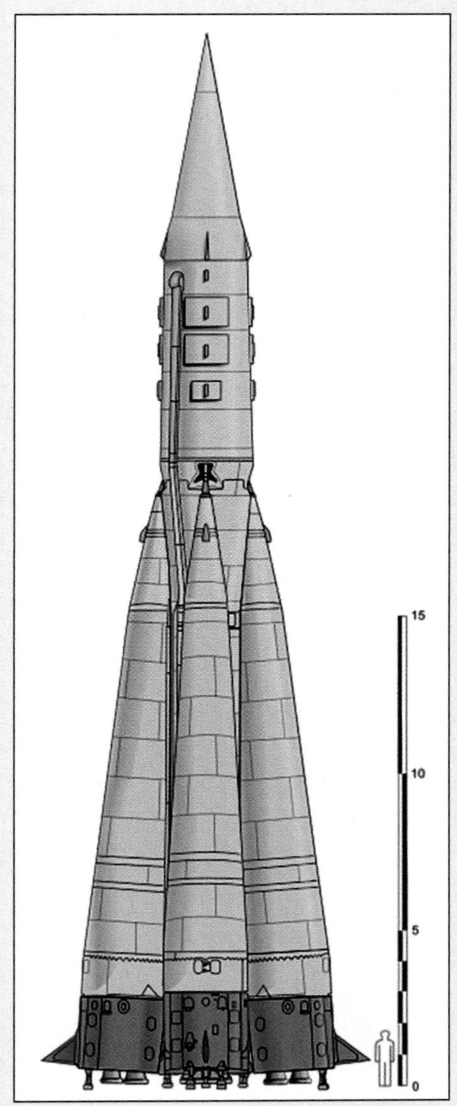

ABOVE: The first Intercontinental Ballistic Missile (ICBM) launched successfully, Russia's R-7 Semyorka began flight operations in 1957. (Heriboto Arribas Abato)

had strategic bombers capable of deploying directly from the United States or from forward bases in the UK and continental Europe. A large force of flight refuelling tankers could give the medium bombers longer range to enter Soviet air space and drop their bombs.

Plans were far along toward a generation of Skybolt stand-off missiles, precursors of the cruise missiles which could be launched from bombers in safer skies far from their targets, allowing the launch aircraft to turn around and escape back to friendly airspace. When the Kennedy administration came in, there were plans for 100 Skybolt missiles to be delivered to the British, at least two of which were to have been carried by each Avro Vulcan B.2.

Skybolt was cancelled in 1962, but the expansion of capability through a Single Integrated Operational Plan (SIOP) gave the incoming Kennedy people grave cause for concern. For Eisenhower, the capacity for destruction of an atomic bomber force was enough to "frighten the devil out of me" and incoming Secretary of Defense Robert McNamara thought the sheer quantity of nuclear weapons envisaged was "fantastic" and disproportionate. SIOP was nothing less than a unified assault on Soviet urban and industrial life intended to "decapitate the leadership," "paralyse the economy," and "render the Sino-Soviet Bloc incapable of continuing war."

"The general impression in the West gave the Soviet Union credit for greater numbers of offensive weapons than was actually the case."

Of increasing concern was the survivability of the President, a matter that had not been seriously considered by either the Truman or Eisenhower administrations – the only ones to have governed the United States during the age of atomic weapons being available. And only since 1949 had there been any other country with an A-bomb. Kennedy was shocked to discover that there was a high probability that the President would be killed in the first wave of Soviet retribution. But that was not the case in Russia.

Probably because of their experience of continental attack during the recent war with Germany, Soviet planners had constructed 2,000 underground bunkers for up to 100,000 officials to protect their leadership. At least 75 emergency relocation centres had been built, some of them several hundred feet deep. Most were for the communist elites, ensuring that the system would survive even at the cost of several millions of ordinary citizens.

Kennedy was briefed on survival plans in the event of a nuclear war and learned that the only relatively safe place in the whole of Washington DC was a shelter beneath the

ABOVE: The United States followed Russia with its own ICBM, the Atlas missile which, like its Soviet equivalent, took several hours to prepare for flight and was thus unsuited to quick-reaction launch. (USAF)

East Wing with very limited bomb-resistance and certainly not to a nuclear attack. There was an alternate command centre located at Fort Ritchie, Maryland with underground facilities but it was not built to withstand a nuclear strike.

Neither was the Cheyenne Mountain Complex in El Paso, Colorado which was linked directly to all the major command units. It too had not been built for nuclear attack although deep inside a natural mountain it was relatively safe, except that the massive 25-tonne doors required an electrically operated hydraulic system easily rendered unusable in the event of a nuclear blast somewhere in the vicinity. In commenting on the vulnerability of all these sites, General Brent Scowcroft quipped that "We must operate on the theory that anything that can be found can be destroyed."

The Kennedy team made the first comprehensive assessment of what was required to bring the nuclear capabilities into full operational control, protected by a more effective system of interlocks. But John and Robert Kennedy were concerned about the vulnerability of the leadership and the effect its decapitation could have on a population hit by a massive Soviet nuclear attack. They learned that if the Kremlin believed that they could limit casualties to less than 50 million, they could conclude "that it might be possible to limit fatalities and damage to much lower levels," according to analyst Desmond Ball. In that event they might believe that a nuclear attack could easily render the US impotent, either to continue to launch reprisals or to retain their country intact.

In 1961, acting on the urgings of McNamara, the Pentagon funded a secret study from the MITRE Corporation to assess the value of building bunkers at depths of 900-3,000m (3,000-10,000ft). Nothing was shown to provide confidence that such facilities would be useful, or even desirable in a nuclear conflict. The President would be incarcerated in a subterranean world provided with stored water and food but with no ability to speak with anyone because the detonation of nuclear warheads would fry the communications equipment.

It became a major point of concern and Kennedy turned to the Pentagon to design and produce a telecommunications system fit for the nuclear age. After finding that far from being on the cutting edge of technology, the Pentagon and its entire apparatus including all the armed services it controlled were running on World War Two equipment. In a frightening admission, Lieutenant General Hillman Dickson said: "we are not well organised to do the same sort of jobs that we did during World War Two…we have a long way to go to get back to that capability".

BELOW: As a back-up to Atlas, the slightly bigger Titan I was also vulnerable, but a second variant had storable propellants and could be launched within minutes of an alert. (USAF)

ABOVE: The secret to survival was to place ICBMs in vertical silos protected by massive concrete doors which could be opened by remote command allowing the rocket to begin its flight. (USAF)

It was these exposed deficiencies that prompted Kennedy to set up the Worldwide Military Command and Control System (WWMCCS). It brought together personnel, equipment, data processing systems and facilities, providing the Secretary of Defense and the White House with accurate and reliable status indicators enabling the President and the Pentagon to get hold of timely reports and detailed intelligence information. It was one of the more important creations by McNamara during his time in government.

A CHANGE IN DIRECTION

With all the information at their disposal, the political and military leadership was hard put to grasp the full significance of all-out nuclear war. Levels of destruction and the number of fatalities would be unimaginable. The transition from the threat of 'massive-retaliation' as a means of containing communism, defined by Secretary of State John Foster Dulles in 1954, to a policy of 'flexible-response', pursued by McNamara in 1961, was a logical move to contain the consequences on an initial exchange of nuclear weapons.

The concept of flexible response had first been presented by General Maxwell Taylor in his 1959 book *The Uncertain Trumpet*, providing a capability to "react across the entire spectrum with anything from general atomic war to infiltrations." Taylor opined that by using atomic weapons on a small scale to stop a war from escalating to an all-out exchange, it would "deter or win quickly limited wars so as to deter general wars…we all want to avoid," adding that he wanted "to respond anywhere, anytime, with weapons and forces appropriate to the situation."

Flexible response was made possible due to the development of much more powerful thermonuclear fusion bombs and by the significant reduction in size that allowed them to be carried by a wider range of delivery systems with higher levels of accuracy. Greatly enhanced explosive yield would allow smaller bombs which if used would imply to an enemy that there was a limited and proportionate response to a pre-emptive attack, delaying escalation.

Flexible-response was accepted by the Kennedy administration as a logical progression, but it built in to a defence strategy the implicit use of nuclear weapons for a wider range of conflicts, from incursions to a strategic, pre-emptive attack. The use of nuclear weapons in tactical situations as well as for strategic applications had always been assumed, but flexible-response embraced a far wider range of options and enshrined it within defence strategy. That threatened to compromise the basic tenet of having nuclear weapons at all, in that it violated the assumption that deterrence would work only if an enemy believed his adversary would unleash destructive power on such a level that its survival was unlikely.

Doctrinally, that uncovered a flaw. Assured destruction left no option for damage limitation and by inference, the limitation to damage on American soil by an enemy operating on the reciprocal principle of 'mutually assured' destruction. That began a debate regarding countervalue (cities and centres of government) and counterforce (military installations and missile sites) targeting. The concept of massive-retaliation had focused on countervalue targets but flexible response and the enhanced accuracy that nuclear missiles and bombers now had allowed a diversion toward a counterforce strategy. If adopted by both sides, that would add another layer of restraint from an all-out exchange by moving the targets away from population centres.

Developed during the 1970s, the Multiple Independently Targeted Re-entry Vehicle (MIRV) consisted of a cylindrical platform on top of the missile which supported three or more separate nuclear warheads, each of which could be released to a different target before it re-entered the atmosphere. At one stroke it multiplied the number of targets that a single missile could hit. Some SLBMs had up to 14 separate warheads. More advanced was the Manoeuvrable Re-entry Vehicle (MARV) which could retarget itself in flight and was deployed with the Pershing II tactical ballistic missile, although several other countries, including Russia, had developed the technology.

ABOVE: The ultimate quick-reaction ICBM, the solid-propellant Minuteman was much smaller and over time replaced the vulnerable Atlas and Titan with their liquid propellant motors. It became the mainstay of the US land-based arsenal throughout the Cold War. (USAF)

> **"The fear in the West of expanding Soviet military capabilities rested largely on the size of the Red Army, most of which was deployed west of the Ural Mountains, and the public perception from their achievements in the Space Race."**

ABOVE: Submarine-launched Ballistic Missile (SLBM) development began with Polaris in the late 1950s and culminates with the nuclear-tipped Trident, now equipping both the US Navy and the Royal Navy with their seaborne strategic deterrent. (Lockheed Martin)

In a further ploy to multiply the number of targets an enemy would need to hit, in the 1970s during the Carter administration a 'racetrack' concept was proposed in which a great number of silos would be needed without increasing the number of expensive missiles deployed. Covered articulated trucks would move the missiles around periodically from silo to silo, confusing the enemy as to which contained missiles, and which were empty. Trucks would feint missile movements in a continuous shell-game. It was cancelled by the Reagan administration, due largely to local opposition, cost, and impracticality.

By the late 1970s, the accuracy of ultra-long range ICBMs had been reduced from several miles to a few hundred feet which was within the levels achieved by manned penetrating bombers. There was now no need for the 'city-busters' of the 1950s, nuclear weapons could be targeted with greater precision. Fewer would be needed, and accuracy meant a more effective way of eliminating the enemy's means of attack. Quite quickly, the race for survival in an all-out nuclear exchange had shifted from a single, all-out nuclear blitz to a selective scaling in the use of nuclear weapons.

That had a consequence which accelerated the arms race and propelled both sides to a massive increase in the number of nuclear weapons held ready for immediate use. At the time of the Cuban missile crisis in October 1962, the United States had 25,540 nuclear warheads, 88% of the world's stockpile, the Russians had 3,346, less than 12%, and the British had 211, less than 1%. But the lessons from the crisis pushed the Soviet Union to build a much stronger nuclear stockpile, reaching

ABOVE: Hungarian revolutionaries arm themselves for a desperate attempt at freeing the country from Soviet occupation. (Jack Metzger)

the inadequacies of the collective socialist economic system and the failed industrial programmes opened avenues for change.

On May 7, 1966, Kádár introduced what has been referred to as the New Economic Mechanism, with farmers again allowed to own the land they worked, military production reduced to 10% of the level it was at prior to 1956 and placed second in priority to food distribution, and a greater liberalisation with increased press freedoms. Hungary became the model for free-market economies aspired to by most of its neighbours, with national pride supporting a growth in consumer demand and the emergence of a new middle-class. With production significantly increased, Moscow sat back and watched as the national economy contributed materially and financially to buck the overall trend in the command-economy of the Soviet Union.

SPRING IN PRAGUE

Although its top-down control over the state and the lives of its citizens stifled latent potential, in Czechoslovakia the process of de-Stalinisation was slow and sluggish. Antonin Novotny became first secretary of the communist party in September 1953 following a succession struggle after the death of Gottwald. His lacklustre effort at satisfying the public hunger for social reforms failed to please either the rest of the national government or Moscow and he was forced to resign on January 5, 1968, leadership going to Alexander Dubček.

Intellectuals and writers had long argued against the system, their views seen by the Party as rebellious and counter-revolutionary. When Dubček came to power he loosened the grip on freedom of speech and also allowed an uncensored political journal to publish alternative views. Its print run soared to over 300,000, the highest of any publication in Europe. Writers, columnists, and political philosophers began to question the history of the country under communism and were joined by radio and TV programmes extending coverage of the debate.

Approval for these limited freedoms came from a few East European countries but the Kremlin leadership was concerned over a repetition of the 1956 Hungarian uprising and met with the Czech leadership to express its concerns. Notwithstanding reassurances, the then Soviet Premier Leonid Brezhnev ordered Russian and Warsaw Pact troops to invade the country and 'liberate' it from anti-socialist threats. This policy of intervention became known as the 'Brezhnev Doctrine', but it would be known nationally and around the world as the 'Prague Spring', in the sense that this immediately preceding period had been the country's 'springtime' of hope.

The invasion took place on August 21, 1968, and passions ran high. Resistance

ABOVE: Russian tanks litter the streets, disabled by lightly armed citizens using hand-held guns and throwing Molotov cocktails. (Foto Fortepan)

BELOW: Forever remembered as the Prague Spring, Russia's heavy-handed approach to unrest at Soviet oppression brought a violent reaction involving the use of tanks and armour to suppress a public uprising during August 1968. (CIA)

took a non-violent form, ordinary citizens climbing on the hulls of Russian tanks and waving national flags. Romanian leader Nicolae Ceausescu protested vehemently in opposition to the Soviet move and both socialist and communist parties around the world expressed their contempt. Underpinning the occupation of Prague, the Brezhnev Doctrine drew fears throughout Eastern Europe that a tougher stance against decentralisation and democratisation would portend other, more violent interventions by Russia. Under it, Brezhnev declared the right of Moscow to suppress any threat to universal socialism and challenges to communist leaders approved of by the Kremlin.

The presence of troops on the streets of Prague brought passive resistance, continual harassment of armed troops, mocked for their acclaimed impertinence in believing they could change everything by the gun. Contrary to a belief in Moscow that the opposition could be quashed in a few days, for eight months the protests endured before a series of political negotiations appeased the crowds gathering in city squares and parks to vent their indignation. Mass emigration began almost immediately the troops arrived and Western airlines smuggled fleeing Czechs desperate to get out aboard scheduled flights leaving for Western Europe and the UK. In April 1969, Dubček was replaced by Gustáv Husák, who restored firm control over the country.

Although ascribed to by history as a 'peaceful' protest, the end of the Prague Spring brought some limited violence, tanks set on fire by outraged citizens and several self-immolated sacrifices in a public outcry of despair at the sustained presence of Soviet troops. The occupying force was diluted with soldiers from other Warsaw Pact countries to retain the fiction that their intervention was for the greater good of the Soviet Union. This belief took hold among those in several East European countries who saw in the Soviet Union a failed model, a political experiment that left people powerless to control their own future.

ABOVE: Romanian communist party leader Nicolae Ceausescu delivers a public speech in Bucharest opposing Russian intervention in Czechoslovakia which had been declared by Moscow as a combined Warsaw Pact effort to prevent subversion. (Romanian National Archives)

The invasion enshrined within Czechoslovak society a discontent that their once-proud country was now merely a satellite of Russia. Not until the collapse of the Soviet Union would the troops pick up their guns and drive away, many back to their own countries now liberated from Soviet rule. As recently as 2015, Russian state TV broadcast a documentary asserting that the occupation of Czechoslovakia had been an essential, defensive measure against an imminent attack by NATO on the Soviet Union, foiled by the Red Army.

The violence of the Hungarian uprising of 1956 and the Czechoslovak rebellion were products of the same symptom, a deep desire on the part of oppressed people to risk all in the pursuit of a free and settled life with some measure of decision over who controlled their potential. It would rise again in the people of Poland and trigger a sequence of events that would bring down the Soviet Union, the Warsaw Pact, and the military occupation of Eastern Europe. And it would end the Cold War. But its ultimate effect was not so evident when that sequence began.

In Poland, reforms introduced by Gomulka during the late 1950s had raised hopes of a better future. Proposed relaxation of constraints on private companies and small industries was stifled by the centralised economic command system, although some progress was made toward market reforms, but these were at odds with the status quo. The desire for separation from Moscow produced astonishing proposals, that Poland, together with West Germany, East Germany and Czechoslovakia establish a nuclear-free zone, for example. After the Berlin Wall cemented divisions between East and West Europe from 1961, Poland's economic plight worsened and public dissatisfaction with the government increased with student demonstrations breaking out in 1968.

The use of Polish troops in suppressing the Prague Spring stimulated additional protests with further societal divisions, countered by efforts from Gomulka for reconciliation with former enemies and the recognition of West Germany's post-war borders. However, as the economic system worsened, general unrest led to strikes and rallies calling for recognition of 'working-class' demands for lower prices and better wages. It did result in those demands being met and for some time tensions were lowered, the intelligentsia usually at the forefront of protest now silent. For the first time, in the 1970s Polish workers could afford a car and a TV set but the global effects of the 1973-74 oil crisis hit consumers and the national budget alike.

ABOVE: Bridging the divide as President Reagan reaches out to shake the hand of a young boy in Red Square, Moscow, during an arms control conference in May 1988. (The White House)

By the early 1980s the economic situation was worse and strikes led by Lech Walesa at the Gdansk shipyard grew far beyond the docks, fanning out across Poland in a fervent demand for change. Social ills and poor wages, appalling health care and the incarceration of political opponents touched off a series of strikes across the country. Lech Walesa became the international symbol for human rights, the call for free elections and democratic government, the very embodiment of civil liberty and unfettered self-determination. All under the name of Solidarity, a word which would be used by other organisations seeking similar rights for decades to come.

When Mikhail Gorbachev became the Soviet premier in March 1985, he gradually introduced reforms under perestroika (restructuring) and glasnost (transparency), raising hope across Eastern Europe that real change was on the way. Preceded by Brezhnev (1964-82), Andropov (1982-84) and Chernenko (1984-85), Gorbachev was the last Soviet leader and his open and honest approach to both politics and the people was seminal. Presiding over the last six years of the USSR, his work and the unifying effect of Lech Walesa inspired other regions struggling to free themselves.

Nowhere was that felt more keenly than in the Baltic states of Lithuania, Latvia, and Estonia, where first Russian and then German troops had occupied them since June 1940 before the Soviet Union swept back through in late 1944. The Germans had conducted mass killings of more than 250,000 Jews from Lithuania and Latvia and during their occupation the Russians deported 200,000 people to the Soviet Union of which 75,000 went to the Gulags.

Throughout the second half of the 1980s, peaceful protests punctuated by the occasional riot, arose throughout the non-Russian republics of the Soviet Union. Gorbachev introduced major reforms and changes were evident across Moscow. Artisans put their products and crafts of all kinds on display for private enterprise and a sense of liberation followed. The Berlin Wall fell on November 1989, with people chanting "Wir wollen raus!" (We want out!). Aspiring to be succession parties, several groups emerged to take over from the USSR, but the collapse came suddenly and with haste when, on December 25, 1991, Gorbachev resigned.

The Cold War began with the Soviet occupation of East European countries and the imposition of totalitarian regimes dictated by Moscow from 1945, denying citizens free choice in their leaders. It is also the place where it ended 45 years later with the collapse from the inside in those same countries operating under one-party systems to the exclusion of free speech as defined in Western Europe and other democratic nations.

ABOVE: Recognising the stifling repression of East European states, Mikhail Gorbachev meets with President Reagan in Geneva, Switzerland, to discuss future possibilities for competitive co-existence and the rights of self-determination. (The White House)

ABOVE: In a small corner of Belarus at a place called Karupaty, crowds gathered in 1989 to contemplate their future in a world where they elect their own leaders and decide their own future. (Valer Palsciuk)

FALLOUT

Every event in the history of the Cold War defined the global stage for what came after the collapse of the Soviet empire. East European countries were liberated for self-determination, in some cases only after 52 years of domination, first by German and then by Russian troops rigidly imposing strict, one-party governments. The euphoria of liberation was mixed, in some cases with hope, in many cases with foreboding. An entire generation had grown up knowing nothing but autocratic rule, never being able to decide their own future, at best making choices over which members of one political party to vote for and at worst no choice at all.

Outside the former Soviet bloc, Western countries wondered what to do with these foundlings of a new post-Cold War world. Opinions differed but other countries would be needed to help them grow again along a very different path. Previously divided into East (German Democratic Republic) and West (Federal Republic of Germany), German reunification was the very embodiment of change and took place between November 1989 and March 1991, October 3, 1990, being the official date when the treaty abolishing the GDR and the FRG signalled the transition and when the two halves of Berlin came together as a single city, the new home of national government.

Many in the former FRG resented the economically impoverished citizens of the GDR, now granted similar social status, and some hostility was expressed by those from the East, previously under the Socialist Unity Party of Germany. Many workers from the East sought jobs in the West in this now unified country previously divided by very different living standards. It took several years for the different social standings between groups to dissipate and some enmity still remains. Germany had paid a high price for the evils of 12 years under a Nazi regime and the 45 years it had suffered as a divided country, its citizens for long almost universally believing that the country was two very different states and would forever remain so.

Almost alone, Britain's Margaret Thatcher and France's Francois Mitterrand vehemently opposed unification and pleaded with Gorbachev to keep Russian troops in the GDR to add a disincentive. But it didn't work, the USSR toppled too quickly for that, and the forces of unification were unstoppable. Neither was there much support in the rest of Europe, but the United States saw great benefit, not least the opportunity to extend its military and politically involved presence further east toward the reconstituted Russia. In settling the new Germany, the border with Poland was set on the Oder-Neisse line.

Now the most powerful nation on Earth, the United States debated the approach it should take to its own position in this monopolar world where Western democracies dominated the geopolitical scene and controlled the international organisations which would preside over an entirely different world order. Some wanted a neutral stance, reaching out to offer Russia the hand of cooperation and unity of purpose, many wanted to capitalise on the defeat of the USSR and embrace those former satellites of Moscow as free countries within the European Union and NATO.

In 1985, on the way to a major summit meeting with Gorbachev, President Reagan penned a note to underpin the way his administration would regard any successes over reducing nuclear weapons and better relations: "Whatever we achieve, we must not

ABOVE: On December 8, 1991, the democratically elected leader of the new Commonwealth of Independent States, Boris Yeltsin (seated second from right) signs the declaration abolishing the Soviet Union. (Novosti)

call it victory." That was repeated by President George H W Bush when the Soviet Union collapsed but there were opposing views about the response, particularly in a report prepared by Paul Wolfowitz, a senior Pentagon official. Wolfowitz prepared guidance for US military plans covering the period 1993 to 1999, completing it on February 18, 1992, the final year of Bush's only term in office.

Its conclusions were firm and set the overriding objective for the United States as preventing "the re-emergence of a new rival, either on the territory of the former Soviet Union or elsewhere... This is a dominant consideration underlying the new regional defense strategy and requires that we endeavor to prevent any hostile power from dominating a region whose resources would, under consolidated control, be sufficient to generate global power."

It also proposed that the US "must account sufficiently for the interests of the advanced industrial nations to discourage them from challenging our leadership or seeking to overturn the established political and economic order. We must maintain the mechanism for deterring potential competitors from even aspiring to a larger regional or global role."

To many, this was a shocking clarion-call for hegemony, tantamount to goals set by the Soviet Union. A leaked draft published by the *New York Times* brought anger among moderates, liberals and the majority of global partners and established Western alliances. Although watered down, the essence of the Wolfowitz report re-emerged after the 9/11 terrorist attacks that in 2001 brought down the Twin Towers in New York and struck the Pentagon.

In reacting to that act of international terrorism, President George W Bush set down guidelines for future American foreign policy, asserting in strident tones that the United States would "Make no distinction between terrorists and the nations that harbor them – and hold both to account." That the country would "Take the fight to the enemy overseas before they can attack us again here at home" and "Confront threats before they fully materialize." More specifically it declared that "our forces will be strong enough to dissuade potential adversaries from pursuing a military build-up in hopes of surpassing, or equalling, the power of the United States," and, in a speech at West Point, a certainty that "America has, and intends to keep, military strengths beyond challenge."

After the Cold War, the foreign policy of the United States retained those principles, and the military capabilities of the country led a reconsolidation in NATO infrastructure and an expansion in its membership. Since the collapse of the USSR, NATO has seen Albania, Bulgaria, the Czech Republic, Estonia, Finland, Hungary, Latvia, Lithuania, Montenegro, North Macedonia, Poland, Romania, Slovakia, and Slovenia

ABOVE: Over time, the removal of the Berlin Wall, the collapse of the Soviet Union and the unification of Germany gave the Brandenburg Gate in the country's new capital special resonance with the post-Cold War world. (Thomas Wolff)

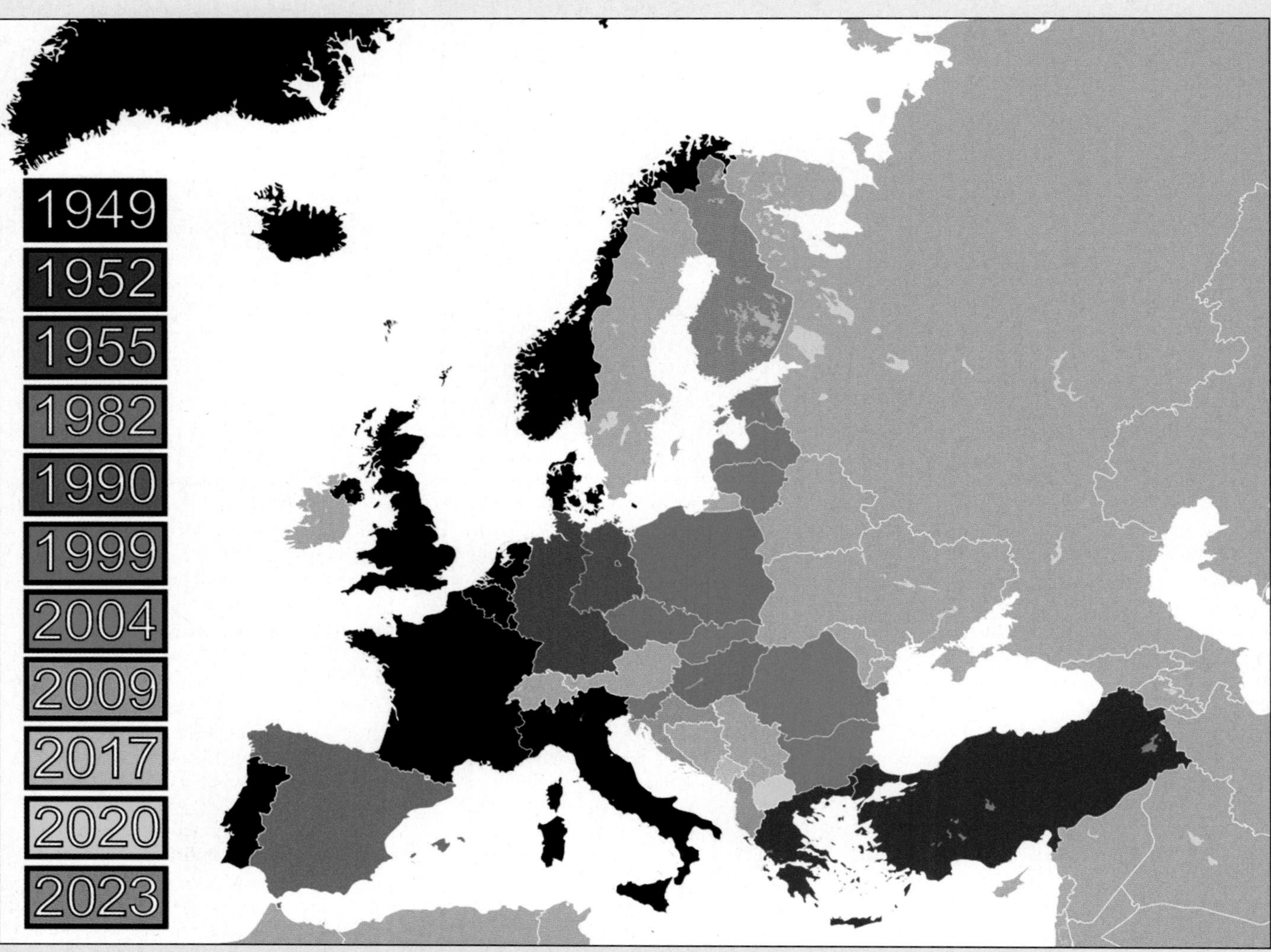

ABOVE: Over time, NATO enlargement would see significant expansion in resources, capabilities, and a potential threat to Russia and to Belarus. (Patrick Neal)

join the military alliance. The Russians saw this as a provocation, claiming that the West was pushing NATO right up to its borders and when the Ukraine made its intentions of eventually joining the military alliance clear, that was used as an excuse for its attack on February 24, 2022.

ABOVE: Paul Wolfowitz crafted a policy document in which the United States would engage with a long-term plan to push the NATO barrier right up to Russia, recruiting East European countries into a collective defence. (US State Department)

UNITING DIVISIONS

The end of the Soviet Union brought little respite in the need for information about threats from potential enemies through several intelligence partnerships that began before the Cold War. In February 1941, a US delegation visited the UK and was shown the codebreaking activity at Bletchley Park. When advised how the US had cracked the Japanese codes, the British shared Enigma secrets and in 1943 formalised the British-USA agreement known as BRUSA. This translated into the UKUSA agreement of March 5, 1946, with Canada joining two years later followed by Australia and New Zealand in 1956, thus forming the 'Five Eyes' intelligence partnership of today.

But the world was not a quiet place and divisions from proxy wars remained. For the communists, the Korean War was seen as a victory. A view shared by China as it increasingly saw itself as the sole custodian of Marxist-Leninism, along with North Korea, which echoed the sentiments of its partner. In March 2023, the most prestigious journal in theoretical strategic policy of the Chinese Communist Party claimed that in the 1950-53 war its army had "defeated the world's No 1 enemy armed to the teeth on the Korean battlefield and performed mighty and majestic battle dramas that shocked the world and caused ghosts and gods to weep."

As recently as 2020, China's leader Xi Jinping claimed that it had been necessary to

> **"Without doubt, the Cold War accelerated the development of both conventional and nuclear weapons."**

intervene as "a war started by the imperialist aggressors reached China's door" and that China had been forced to send "a message they will understand." Xi reminded his audience that China had imposed "an earth-shaking epic, defeating an enemy rich in steel but weak in will." The Korean War is today regarded, and taught in China as a seminal moment that, although exhausted by the intensity of the civil war that brought it to power, in its weakened form China had forced upon its opponents a stalemate that in its own interpretation was a victory, a pause and not an end ratified by an armistice.

The Korean War greatly influenced the way Britain saw itself and was seen by the world. At the time, Britain was unable to mount a major campaign on its own, while still holding fast to the last vestiges of an imperial past. With neither the money nor the manpower to project power and geopolitical influence, for Britain the Korean War signalled a sequence of events that would forever change its global role, making it more dependent than ever on collaboration and cooperation with the United States and at the early stages of the Common Market and a European Union.

Arguably the most quoted conflict of the period, Vietnam took the greatest toll on human life and saw the greatest destruction of land and property since World War Two, causing environmental damage that will take decades to ameliorate. Today, those countries are free from war and welcome tourists, but the scars are there to remind visitors of days when an ideological war was fought and lost by those who claimed hold on stopping the dominoes falling.

ABOVE: Key players in the readjustment of Europe (from left): Vladimir Putin (Russia), Emmanuel Macron (France), Angela Merkel (Germany) and Volodymyr Zelensky (Ukraine). (The Kremlin)

The development of a global community of countries for trade and economic development was a result of World War Two, a product of the capitalist system for profit and private ownership, mobility lubricated by reduced regulatory structures and a light touch on constraining international banking and global money markets. The communist 'world' ran on completely different principles, oiled by top-down controls and centralised management, national ownership tightening constraints on private enterprise and individual entrepreneurial contributions.

The two systems connected but only at the periphery. The capitalist countries in the West saw great increases in living standards, wages, expansion of the middle classes and a vibrant domestic and international market for goods and services. The communist countries had no middle class other than those groups patronised and held up with privileges doled out by the state, lacking a vibrant domestic consumer market and stifling incentive and opportunity. Except to those deemed by the state apparatus to benefit the Marxist-Leninist ethic.

Freedoms acquired by East European countries formerly under Soviet controls eagerly accepted capitalist principles and grew their economies proportionately. Political leadership was now a more complex and nuanced process, several years required to adapt to ways and means unfamiliar to a generation sustained by the state apparatus. In general, there was a burst of enthusiastic connection with Western markets, their citizens engaging on a wide range of commercial and business platforms. In so many ways, these once inaccessible

BELOW: The 'Five Eyes' intelligence partnership of the US, UK, Canada, Australia, and New Zealand revives the original BRUSA agreement of 1941, Canada's Communications Security Establishment being situated in Ottawa. (Eshko Timiou)

ABOVE: On May 21, 2014, China and Russia signed a 30-year deal on the supply of natural gas with premiers Putin (left) and Xi (right) looking on, expanding in recent years as Russia deems Europe 'unfriendly'. (The Kremlin)

countries embraced what to them was a new and exciting, if not a challenging world also fraught with danger and potential disaster.

For Russians, the opportunity to take charge of government departments and agencies across the country brought turbulent times. The folly of pitching full-tilt into a sometimes violently unstable commercial and banking environment provided instant and personal wealth for individual opportunists who displayed little responsibility toward their country, for fellow players in a very unfamiliar system or provision for an uncertain future. This pitched the Russian economy into a period of political and economic uncertainty, leaving many with a nostalgia for the old ways and a bitter disregard for the lauded opportunities they were seduced into practicing.

Attracted to a coalition of countries which they were encouraged to join, the establishment of the European Union on November 1, 1993, was both timely and opportunistic, providing a safe-haven for countries unschooled in the larger world beyond what had once been the 'Iron Curtain'. The political unification of Europe was seen by several countries as a price worth paying for an inseparable and interdependent continent in which war between the member states is no longer possible.

> "Britain's Margaret Thatcher and France's Francois Mitterrand vehemently opposed unification and pleaded with Gorbachev to keep Russian troops in the GDR."

Supporters of the EU and the price of membership reflect on the cost to Germany for its own national unity and believe it to be a worthwhile investment. Not a price but an insurance policy for shared responsibilities as a separate set of collegiate but democratically independent countries. When the two halves of this once-divided nation came together, the exchange rate between the two currencies was equalled, costing the united Germany an average €100bn a year for two decades while absorbing the economic losses caused by achieving parity between the once-impoverished East and the more prosperous West.

Opponents of the EU are concerned about the dominant part played by the established leaders of West European development since World War Two – principally, France and Germany – with a disproportionately reduced 'voice' for the small nations. When the UK departed the EU on January 31, 2020, a number of member-states said that they had lost a voice for their cause, not least among that group being the Baltic countries and some of the smaller states for whom the British had frequently sided and trumpeted their apparent plight in Brussels. Others complain about the lack of sovereignty but former East European countries previously under orders from Moscow find common cause with Winston Churchill's comment about democracy being the worst of all systems, until the others are looked at in detail!

PLOUGHSHARES INTO SWORDS

Without doubt, the Cold War accelerated the development of both conventional and nuclear weapons, the Korean War propelling Western nations to reverse demobilisation and increase defence budgets. New and fearsome weapons built arsenals of unprecedented might and capability, some of that vented on the hapless victims of proxy wars and peripheral conflicts. It set as a fixture the dramatic increase in procurement and production that ensued and in the deployment of new technologies. Although defence budgets came down for several decades after the Cold War, they are on the rise again as a new geopolitical map emerges with the axis of attention shifting from Europe to southeast Asia. The number of states with nuclear weapons is increasing and the number of weapons held by the nuclear powers is growing again.

Diminished as a military power by fewer resources in the decades since the end of the USSR, Russia has failed to maintain its technological capabilities, and this has been seen in its recent conflicts. Not a direct result of the Cold War, its engagement in Afghanistan between 1979 and 1989 was largely to suppress the Mujahideen fighters

ABOVE: Russian armoured vehicles and tanks move in the Donetsk region of Ukraine. Russia's military operation in Ukraine since February 24, 2022, has shown the inability of its forces to overwhelm Western military equipment. (Mstyslav Chernov)

BELOW: In preparation for placing spacemen on the Moon by 2028, China is engaged in a vigorous programme of unmanned exploration, represented here by Change-4 on the far side of the lunar surface imaged by the Yutu-2 roving vehicle. (CSNA)

trying to bring down the Soviet-backed government, which had itself been installed by coercion and intrigue. That war resulted in around 90,000 Soviet casualties and depleted capabilities from which it took a long time to recover.

The population of the Russian Federation is now 143 million compared with 286 million when the Soviet Union collapsed and that significantly reduces its ability to add conscripts to the fighting in Ukraine. In that regard, the present state of Russia's military is a direct result of the war in Afghanistan, which never did allow sufficient resources for re-equipping the armed forces prior to the collapse of the USSR. But the core of Russia's present military action in Ukraine is a direct result of Vladimir Putin's desire to get back territories lost during World War One and after the collapse of the Soviet Union.

Another product of the Cold War, the Space Race with Russia was shaped by Eisenhower so as to encourage a positive view of the programme. In setting up NASA as a civilian government agency open to scrutiny and to sharing information it obtained, Eisenhower achieved a master-stroke of public persuasion. When the US Air Force had controlled previous space launches the press were open-handed and judged, or ridiculed, projects in much the same way they viewed any government programme – with a touch of cynicism born of objectivity.

When NASA embraced the media and brought them closer to what was going on, bombarding them with manuals, press handouts, a limitless supply of photographs and open access to astronauts and managers, photographers, reporters, editors, and publishers were stricken with 'go fever', even when public opinion polls showed disapproval for big-scale government space spending. Under Kennedy and Johnson, the space programme grew to embrace Moon landings and space stations, the same persuasive access presenting a highly positive view from both print and electronic media. But when the high-spending years of the Apollo programme went, the agency was left with a budget around one-third the level it had during peak years.

After the collapse of the Soviet Union, the United States and its partners Japan, the European Space Agency, and Canada invited the Russians to pool their extensive knowledge and join them in what became the International Space Station (ISS). Assembled partly by Russian rockets and station modules and supplied for many years by Soyuz spacecraft ferrying crew members back and forth, the ISS has been permanently manned since 2000 and is destined to remain so for another 10 years. The turbulent and frequently fractious competition of the Cold War years evolved into one of the biggest international engineering projects of all time, achieved only through the cooperation of people from very different cultures across the globe.

Since Russia's invasion of Ukraine began in February 2022, US and European cooperation has been withdrawn from the ISS and the Russians have turned to China, forging new links for joint ventures in space. While they maintain a presence on the ISS, it is highly unlikely that this will be continued when the big orbiting station is de-orbited in 2033. The Russians and the Chinese are already working on manned missions to the lunar surface where semi-permanent, sustainable bases are expected to be set up. China has made strong statements that their astronauts will be on the Moon by 2028 and this has spurred US plans for a similar capability in the Artemis programme, with the same international partners, except for the Russians.

The reorientation in geopolitical alignment brought about by China's exponential growth and sanctions on Russia for its military action against Ukraine has re-orientated the alignment of many countries, with China, Russia, North Korea, and Iran involved in sharing military equipment including rockets and missiles. The Western group of nations including the United States, the UK, Australia, New Zealand, and the European Union are the new alignment which is likely to persist throughout the next decade at least. New moves are afoot on the geopolitical chessboard and new players are joining the game, but nobody quite knows what those moves will be. What is unequivocal is that all that happens today is a direct result of the Cold War.

ABOVE: Sharing a meal together, 13 members of the crew aboard the International Space Station with astronauts from Canada, the US, Japan, Russia, and Europe, a microcosm of international partnership which many of its citizens anticipated the post-Cold War world would be like. (NASA)

THE COLD WAR TIMELINE

The following dates mark significant events or episodes in the Cold War between 1945 and 1991, some of which are not mentioned in the previous chapters.

FEBRUARY 4-11, 1945
Yalta Conference is held in the Crimea to agree free elections across Eastern Europe.

APRIL 12, 1945
President Roosevelt dies and is succeeded by his deputy Harry S Truman.

JULY 17 - AUGUST 2, 1945
The Potsdam Conference is held.

AUGUST 6, 1945
Atom bomb dropped on Hiroshima followed by Nagasaki three days later.

SEPTEMBER 2, 1945
Japan signs the declaration of surrender, ending World War Two.

MARCH 5, 1946
Winston Churchill declares that an Iron Curtain has descended across Europe.

MARCH 12, 1947
The Truman Doctrine is announced, covering aid for countries to prevent them falling into the hands of the Soviet Union.

OCTOBER 5, 1947
Russia sets up the COMINFORM organisation to control political parties and national leadership in East European countries.

FEBRUARY 25, 1948
Communists take control of Czechoslovakia in a bloodless coup.

APRIL 3, 1948
The Marshall Plan is signed under which the US will eventually provide $12.4bn in aid to West European countries.

JUNE 12, 1948
Communist head Mátyás Rákosi becomes de-facto leader of Hungary.

JUNE 18, 1948
A communist uprising in British-run Malaya starts in a conflict lasting 12 years and becomes the only successful counter-insurgency campaign of the Cold War.

JUNE 24, 1948
Stalin orders the Berlin Blockade in which food and fuel can only be delivered from the West by air.

APRIL 4, 1949
North Atlantic Treaty Organisation (NATO) is formed as a mutual support alliance pledging military aid for any member state attacked by another country.

MAY 11, 1949
End of the Berlin Blockade as Russia opens the access routes by land.

AUGUST 29, 1949
Russia detonates its first atomic bomb.

ABOVE: US Army tanks and infantry move across a frozen Korean landscape. (US Army)

SEPTEMBER 15, 1949
Konrad Adenauer becomes the first chancellor of the Federal Republic of (West) Germany.

OCTOBER 7, 1949
Russia declares East Germany to be the German Democratic Republic and its capital East Berlin.

OCTOBER 16, 1949
The leader of the Greek communist party Nikos Zachariadis declares an end to the civil war which marks the first suppression of communist aggression.

MARCH 11, 1950
Chiang Kai-shek establishes the capital for the Republic of China in Taipei, Taiwan, after the party is driven out of the declared People's Republic of China by its communist leader Mao Zedong.

APRIL 7, 1950
At the US State Department, Paul Nitze issues NSC-68, a policy advocating containment of communism.

JUNE 25, 1950
Communist forces from North Korea invade South Korea beginning the Korean War as a United Nations resolution calls upon nations to evict the invaders.

JULY 4, 1950
UN forces arrive in South Korea and engage with communist forces.

SEPTEMBER 15, 1950
UN forces spearheaded by the US military land on the coast of Korea at Inchon.

MARCH 29, 1951
In the US, illegals Julius and Ethel Rosenberg are convicted of spying for the Russians from 1942 and executed on June 19, 1953.

FEBRUARY 6, 1952
Britain's King George VI dies and is succeeded by Queen Elizabeth II who will reign over the UK and the Commonwealth for 70 years and six months.

OCTOBER 3, 1952
The UK detonates its first atomic bomb, making Britain the third nuclear power.

NOVEMBER 1, 1952
The US detonates its first thermonuclear bomb in the Ivy Mike test.

ABOVE: Nuclear test heralds a new age of atomic warfare. (US Army)

JANUARY 20, 1953
President Dwight D Eisenhower is sworn in to office with John Foster Dulles as secretary of state.

MARCH 5, 1953
Josef Stalin dies, signalling a softening of controls and policies as a power struggle develops.

JUNE 17, 1953
Russian troops quell uprising in East Germany.

JULY 27, 1953
The Korean War ends with an armistice but no peace treaty to the present day.

SEPTEMBER 7, 1953
Nikita Khrushchev becomes leader of the communist party in Russia.

JANUARY 21, 1954
The US Navy launches the USS *Nautilus*, the first submarine powered by a nuclear reactor.

MARCH 13, 1954
The KGB is formed out of the pre-existing NKVD for Russia's intelligence and national security service.

MAY 7, 1954
French forces in Vietnam are defeated at the battle of Dien Bien Phu and withdraw.

MAY 5, 1955
The US military occupation of West Germany ends and is followed by a similar move by Britain and France with West Germany joining NATO four days later.

FEBRUARY 25, 1956
Khrushchev makes a speech condemning the 'cult of personality' and begins a process of de-Stalinisation which brings some opposition.

OCTOBER 23, 1956
The Hungarian revolution begins but Russian troops quell the uprising.

OCTOBER 29, 1956
France, Britain, and Israel attack Egypt in an attempt to overthrow Abdul Nasser, a failed effort known as the 'Suez Crisis'.

MAY 15, 1957
Britain detonates its first hydrogen bomb.

AUGUST 31, 1957
Malaysia gains independence from Britain but the communist insurgency lasts a further three years.

OCTOBER 1, 1957
The US Air Force Strategic Air Command begins a constant round-the-clock alert which will continue until 1991.

OCTOBER 4, 1957
Russia launches Sputnik 1, the world's first artificial satellite.

NOVEMBER 7, 1957
President Eisenhower begins a campaign to build nuclear fall-out shelters.

NOVEMBER 15, 1957
Khrushchev challenges America to a 'shooting match' to prove that Russia has superiority in rockets and missiles.

DECEMBER 16-19, 1957
NATO holds its first summit in Paris, the first time all its leaders have gathered together since its formation in 1949.

JULY 14, 1958
A military coup in Iraq topples the monarch and establishes a pro-Soviet regime.

ABOVE: European campaigns against the prolific spread of nuclear weapons. (Ark of Lanzo del Vasto)

JANUARY 1, 1959
In a revolution, Fidel Castro becomes head of Cuba and inspires similar attempts at regime-change across Latin America.

SEPTEMBER 15, 1959
In the first visit by a Russian leader to the United States. Khrushchev begins a 13-day state tour.

FEBRUARY 13, 1960
France detonates its first atom bomb.

MAY 1, 1960
US pilot Francis Gary Powers is shot down in his U-2 spy plane and is put on trial in Moscow.

JANUARY 20, 1961
John F Kennedy becomes President of the United States.

APRIL 12, 1961
Russia's Yuri Gagarin becomes the first human in space.

APRIL 17, 1961
Bay of Pigs fiasco in which a CIA backed invasion of Cuba fails.

JUNE 4, 1961
Kennedy meets Khrushchev in Vienna, Austria.

AUGUST 13, 1961
Construction of the Berlin Wall begins.

FEBRUARY 10, 1962
US U-2 pilot Powers is exchanged for Russian spy Rudolf Abel.

OCTOBER 16, 1962
The Russians secretly begin installing military bases and prepare to deploy nuclear weapons on Cuba before agreeing to remove them.

AUGUST 5, 1963
The US, Russia and the UK sign a partial test ban treaty prohibiting nuclear weapons tests above ground.

NOVEMBER 22, 1963
President Kennedy is shot and killed in Dallas, Texas, and is succeeded by Lyndon B Johnson.

AUGUST 2, 1964
US ship is allegedly attacked by communist North Vietnam, triggering a response which escalates the Vietnam War.

OCTOBER 14, 1964
Leonid Brezhnev succeeds Khrushchev.

OCTOBER 16, 1964
China detonates its first atomic bomb and its first hydrogen bomb on June 17, 1967.

JANUARY 24, 1965
Winston Churchill dies.

JANUARY 5, 1968
The 'Prague Spring' begins in Czechoslovakia but is suppressed by Russian tanks.

JANUARY 20, 1969
Richard Nixon becomes President of the United States.

JULY 20, 1969
Neil Armstrong and Buzz Aldrin land on the Moon.

FEBRUARY 21, 1972
First visit by a US President to communist China.

DECEMBER 18, 1972
Nixon declares a massive bombing campaign in North Vietnam to force the North Vietnamese to peace talks.

AUGUST 9, 1974
Richard Nixon resigns as President and is succeeded by Gerald Ford.

APRIL 30, 1975
The fall of Saigon as American forces withdraw from South Vietnam.

JANUARY 20, 1977
Inauguration of Jimmy Carter as US President.

JANUARY 1, 1979
The US and China formalise diplomatic relations.

DECEMBER 24, 1979
Russians invade Afghanistan, ending a period of détente.

JULY 3, 1980
The CIA begins arming Afghan Mujahideen against Russian occupation.

JANUARY 20, 1981
Ronald Reagan inaugurated as US President.

SEPTEMBER 26, 1983
A Russian missile officer correctly judges that an early-warning system showing multiple US nuclear missiles launched against the Soviet Union to be false, averting a global nuclear exchange.

MARCH 11, 1985
Mikhail Gorbachev becomes leader of the Soviet Union, meets with Reagan on November 21.

JUNE 12, 1987
During a speech in Berlin, Reagan appeals to Gorbachev to "Tear down this Wall".

MAY 15, 1988
Russian troops begin withdrawing from Afghanistan.

DECEMBER 7, 1988
Gorbachev pledges that never again will Soviet troops intervene in East European countries.

JANUARY 20, 1989
George H W Bush inaugurated as US President.

DECEMBER 16, 1989
A revolution begins in Romania which will overthrow Ceausescu and execute him six days later.

JULY 10, 1991
Boris Yeltsin elected President of Russia, resigning on December 31, 1999, and succeeded by Vladimir Putin.

DECEMBER 25, 1991
The Soviet Union is dissolved, ending the Cold War.

ABOVE: US President Ronald Reagan (left) and Soviet Premier Mikhail Gorbachev sign a nuclear arms agreement in 1988. (The White House)